The African Nations
and World Solidarity

The
African Nations
And
World Solidarity

Mamadou Dia

Translated from the French by
Mercer Cook

FREDERICK A. PRAEGER, Publisher

New York

BOOKS THAT MATTER

First published in France in 1960 under the title of
Nations Africaines et Solidarité Mondiale
by Presses Universitaires de France

Published in the United States of America in 1961
by Frederick A. Praeger, Inc., Publisher
64 University Place, New York 3, N.Y.

Library of Congress Catalog Card Number: 61–17815

The African Nations and World Solidarity
is published in two editions:

A Praeger Paperback (PPS–61)
A clothbound edition

Printed in the United States of America

To the Memory of My Children,
FATOU, AIDA, EL-HADJ,
too quickly torn away from paternal affection

FOREWORD

THIS IS A courageous book. In their desire to appear infallible, political leaders seldom admit their mistakes, except perhaps in reminiscences after retirement. Here, however, we find a responsible African statesman—the Prime Minister of Senegal —publicly acknowledging the miscalculations that culminated in the dissolution of the Mali Federation on August 20, 1960. "Taking our ideal for a reality," he writes in the Epilogue, "we thought we had only to condemn territorialism and its natural product, micronationalism, to overcome them and assure the success of our chimerical undertaking." The author even admits that the Senegalese people diagnosed the viability of the Federation more accurately than did the leaders.

In the present African context, in the present world context, it takes courage to voice unpleasant truths. It is not easy for an official of an emergent African nation to view colonialism objectively; to advocate economic solidarity with the former Metropole and the rest of the world; to refuse to govern by anti-imperialist slogans. Nor is it easy—or popular —for a nationalist leader to point out the dangers of narrow nationalism; to avoid extremism; to recommend a program of austerity and co-operation.

Like most African leaders, Mamadou Dia is a socialist;

he rejects capitalism as outmoded, inhuman, and short-sighted. The recently liberated masses of the underdeveloped countries tend to identify capitalism with colonialism. But the African socialism proposed by Mamadou Dia and Senegalese President Léopold Sédar Senghor is a far cry from the system practiced by the Soviet Union. One reason for their rejection of the Russian model is its godlessness. "The Soviet Union," said Mamadou Dia on his return from Moscow, "has succeeded in building socialism, but at the sacrifice of religion, of the soul."[1]

In this volume, Prime Minister Dia makes a convincing case against Communism on other grounds. He readily acknowledges the economic and industrial progress achieved in Soviet Russia, but regrets that so little of it is shared by other members of the Soviet bloc. His analysis of the satellite countries' economies reveals a dependence strangely similar to that of underdeveloped African territories, with comparable disparities and imbalance. Furthermore, he warns that the aid accorded emergent African nations by Marxists "who pose as champions of African nationalism" is often the result of strategic and tactical considerations. With admirable foresight, he announces that Africans will not accept second-class nationhood, and he predicts "merciless struggles" between "today's protégé and his protector," the former rebels against "Communist imperialism." In this connection, he asks a key question: "Does imperialism cease to be an evil and suddenly become acceptable because one has transferred from the capitalist to the socialist camp?"

It would be misleading, however, to describe the volume

[1] Léopold Sédar Senghor, *African Socialism* (New York: American Society of African Culture, 1959), p. 29.

as a post-mortem on the Federation of Mali or as a mere condemnation of a given economic and political system. Mamadou Dia is motivated by a more constructive objective: he is writing to lay the foundation for a new Senegal, a new Africa, a new world. The solution to Africa's economic problems lies neither in continued Balkanization nor in the intensification of the Cold War. "Positive neutralism, truly neutral and really positive," cannot be achieved by micronationalisms and micronations. The alternative is a solidarity that will link African nations and proceed "by concentric circles" to include the entire world.[2] This theory of mutual development, inspired by Professor François Perroux, one of France's leading economists, provides the focal point for the entire book. Some may judge it to be too idealistic; others, too theoretical. We would remind the former that a world without ideals is a world without hope. For those who find the volume too theoretical, we would quote a statement from Gunnar Myrdal's *Economic Theory and Under-Developed Regions:* "It must be said, however, that theory is indispensable for scientific work. Theory is necessary not only to organize the findings of research so that they make sense but, more basically, to determine what questions are to be asked."[3]

Mamadou Dia's theory has enabled him to pose the right questions and to suggest answers that merit the careful consideration of men of good will everywhere. Volumes like *The African Nations and World Solidarity* will help to make the voice of a progressive, moderate, independent Africa heard above the roar of the Congo and the rumble of propaganda.

[2] An initial step in this direction was the formation, in March, 1961, of a group of twelve French-speaking African nations and Madagascar at Yaoundé, Cameroun.

[3] (London: Duckworth & Co., 1957), p. 160.

Foreword

The African Nations and World Solidarity, Mamadou Dia's fourth book, was preceded by *Réflexions sur l'économie de l'Afrique noire* (Paris: Editions Africaines, 1953); *Contribution à l'étude du mouvement coopératif en Afrique noire* (Paris: Editions Africaines, 1957); and *L'Economie africaine, études et problèmes nouveaux* (Paris: Presses Universitaires de France, 1957).

For assistance with various terms and some of the footnotes, we are deeply indebted to Professor François Perroux, M. T. Seck (Senegalese Consul in Paris), M. Colin (President Dia's *Directeur de Cabinet*), and M. T. D. Thiam. Whatever errors remain in the text are the sole responsibility of the translator.

MERCER COOK

CONTENTS

Contents

I

The Revolt of the Proletarian Nations
or
The Twentieth-Century Revolution

1

TOWARD A NEW DEFINITION OF NATION

ONE NEED NOT BE a prophet to predict that in the coming years, the arrival at the United Nations of a wave of young nations, most of them African, will continue to shake the world's equilibrium. This prospect, which causes some uneasiness—admitted or not—is attributable to a nationalism over which Western Europe has lost its monopoly. Nevertheless, the nationalism that today is liberating overseas territories owes much to the West, especially to Europe, mother of nationalism and, at the same time, by a strange destiny, mother of colonialism. By linking a colonizing mission to its national vocation, the West, or more precisely Europe, provided the impact, with results that have not always been a negative influence.

Analyzing the different phases in the economic growth of nations, W. W. Rostow, an economic historian, rightly emphasizes the positive role played by colonialism in the transforming process that prepares for the take-off and subsequently for the progress toward maturity. Willingly or unwillingly, colonization carries the germ of liberation, by virtue of the transformations that it involves, the changes it introduces in ideas, institutions, and mores, and the basic services it implants, indispensable for the activity of the colonial so-

3

ciety, which is itself obliged to evolve from the traditional to the transitional stage.

Let us not expect colonization to be more than it could possibly become, namely, an ethic. Let us agree to judge it by its results and we shall have to admit that, along with its ravages, colonization—any colonization—makes some favorable contributions. On this point, the opinion of the political historian cannot objectively differ from that of the economic historian. African civilizations have known periods of decline during which atrocious feudalisms have reigned, after eras of splendor sustained by an impeccable state organization. Why deny it, in the face of the most patent historical truth? Human societies and nations are similar: they get the fate that they deserve. African nations, like all nations torn by dissension, anarchy, and neglect of the collective welfare, have become easy prey. Colonization has provided the shock that awakened them and inspired a new spirit. It is not paradoxical to contend that colonization engendered nationalism, not only that of clans and tribes, but also doctrinal, unifying nationalism, which transforms the struggle of colonized nations into a struggle on a world-wide scale.

But how can we speak of African nations while African nationalism is still at the revolutionary stage; while it has not yet emancipated more than a tiny fraction of the population; while the few states that have been created are for the most part unable to assume national vocations? This is the moment, we believe, to attack the concept of "nation" by which Western historians tend to make of it a special "category," a notion peculiar to their society or to Western-type societies in general. Renan stepped out of character in his famous lecture when he affirmed that the nation was not only a historical fact, not just a group of men, a territory, a tradition, a "soul," but the spiritualized version of these different material elements, the whole of which is oriented toward the common good of the group, of humanity. What must be stressed in this definition is that instead of being a static, definitive state, the nation is rather an affirmation, a perpetual movement, an unfinished construction. Placing oneself in Renan's train of thought, one might define the nation as a collective vocation, depending on a common scale of values, common institutions, and, finally, common aims.

Thus we must discard racist theories that claim to base the national vocation on the race or the people. These are mere biological elements, the components of a vocation, not the vocation itself. "To be what nature makes of us is not the same as having a vocation."[1] Increasingly numerous are the examples of historically and ethnically heterogeneous groups that share a collective national vocation. It is to be hoped that this process may become general, thus settling certain frightful dramas and making new nations centers of humanism, by the diversity of the human elements assembled. If they are willing to seize this opportunity, the emergent nations can make an invaluable contribution to the cause of world civilization. Imagine for a single instant all the power of conciliation, concord, and fraternity accumulated in *the dynamic notion of an Algerian nation* conceived and accepted as in Brazil, where the German immigrants have blended into the national unity.

As a vocation, the nation cannot be a rigid framework for activities: it is a stimulus. Its frontiers cannot be those of

[1] F. Perroux, *La Nation est une vocation,* lecture delivered at the Collège de France.

dwarf states that try to atomize it, to divide it against itself and so guarantee its failure. We must always remember this in order not to create static situations or compromise the nation's possibilities of expansion by obstructing the future. This is how we must interpret Péguy's magnificent statement: "The nation is a mission." Certainly not the mission of devouring others, of suppressing other vocations, or of subordinating them to one's own, but that of permitting, by peaceful radiation, the accomplishment of the largest possible and most human collective vocation. This is why any qualifications that one tries to attach to the right of self-determination seem to us as dangerous as the negation of that principle. They destroy the national reality by introducing a process of disintegration and making their major premise a historical error that places on the same plane elements as diversified as nation, people, and territory.

It is perfectly obvious that the nation as a collective vocation within African dimensions necessarily groups diverse countries and peoples. Hence the stupidity of certain border disputes that seem to excite African or Arab leaders who lack neither culture nor political realism. They act as if it were a question of fixing a definite form to this vast movement that will continue to seek an equilibrium not yet attained. They act as if it were a matter of launching a competition between national vocations, while nations large or small, rich or poor, in Africa and elsewhere, have real value only as instruments of world solidarity. In short, they act as if the nation were an absolute, not—as it is by definition—a contingent reality, with changing frontiers. This is particularly true of the emergent nations.

History furnishes unforgettable examples. The Venetian

and Florentine national vocations, although clearly expressed, were no less happily merged in a wider and more authentically national collective vocation—the Italian vocation. The states emerging in our time have the right to set territorial limits for themselves and to remain within those limits. They would be wrong to confuse these with the boundaries of the emergent nation or nations and to try to impose their dimensions on the latter. On the other hand, one cannot refuse the various national vocations the right to exist, on the pretext of unification or supranationality. It seems evident to us that here one must be careful not to adopt the idolatry that totalitarian regimes propose—interpreting the nation grossly without pushing the analysis any further. Western socialists who urge colonized people to abandon their national vocation in favor of socialism—without, however, renouncing their own nationalism—have to be shown the firm desire for nationhood.

Despite what is heard or written in the name of pure doctrine, nothing is less certain than the contention that class is a higher form of integration than nation, and sufficient in itself for the realization of the common good. The formation of proletarian nations on the imperialistic model is surely the most forceful argument against the alleged power attributed to class and the illusions that many try to maintain concerning it. Pierre Moussa claims that one of the essential factors impeding the revalorization of the prices of raw materials from the *Tiers-Monde*[2]—and we shall see that this problem is basic for the proletariat of those countries—is the fact that the

---

[2] *Tiers-Monde* is an expression currently used in French to designate the so-called underdeveloped countries. It is based on the assumption that the world at the moment is divided into two camps, with the underdeveloped countries constituting a third part. (We are indebted to Professor François Perroux for this note.—Tr.)

7

Western working class—after bitter, violent struggles, of course —turns to its advantage an important part of the profits extracted by the capitalists. This example suffices to illustrate once and for all the inadequacy of class to realize a vertical socialist integration in the concrete domain of wages and living standards, and consequently, on the moral plane, its total inability to embody such spiritual values as justice, equality, and fraternity. In the present context of historical development, it is clear that the proletarian nations would strike a foolish bargain if they renounced their own vocations for an integration that the Western nations, of whatever bloc, do not yet seem ready for. In this respect, all the nationalists of the different underdeveloped countries will endorse the following declaration of the Lebanese socialist Clovis Maksoud:

> The nationalist struggle is not a backward step that lessens the universality of the Arab-socialist ideal. Nationalism in the context of the Arab world is the force that seeks to raise the Arabs to a rank where they will be totally engaged in universal humanist movements and where their support of internationalist objectives will be more positive and more concrete. To ask progressive Arabs to accept the current interpretation that Western socialists attach to nationalism is to invite them to act in isolation. In fact, this is asking them to entrust the leadership of the inevitable struggle for unity and liberation to opportunistic, illogical politicians, who would turn the legitimate demands of the people to ends harmful to the cause of social, economic, and political democracy in the Middle East.[3]

Concluding this brief analysis, we readily see that the classic theories about nation, including that of scientific social-

[3] "Socialistes arabes et Occidentaux," *Cahiers internationaux,* May, 1956.

ism, must at least be revised. The nations of the twentieth century are no longer defined by a historical context, by material supports, by the homogeneity of environment, of culture, but much more so by potentialities, by possibilities of synthesis, and, at the same time, by the homogeneity of the elements to be regrouped. The U.S.S.R., India, the forthcoming Confederation of Independent States of the Franco-African Community offer, each in its fashion, instructive examples. It is the mutual respect of national vocations, of national cultures, of national personalities that assures the success of the common undertaking. Far from being an obstacle to the latter or an inhibiting force against integration, the nation-vocation is characteristic of them.

We must remember that while no nation is valid without morality, it certainly cannot be valid without economic and technical efficiency in this cruel world. The nationalism of colonial and former colonial territories, if it is to attain the desired result, owes it to itself to be an active, constructive nationalism, determined to transform a state of revolt into an effective revolution. In this light, the concept of "African nations" finds theoretical and practical justification, even in the absence of an impressive past (and we know that this is not the case), even in the absence of perfectly organized institutions. What matters primarily is the consciousness of being, the will to be born, to participate in world growth, and to require justice of other nations. Such is the meaning of the revolution that is being waged before our eyes and that henceforth will take the initiative away from the West.

Nationalism in this sense is something quite different from a theory founded on racial or religious ideology. Nationalism with a racial or religious basis is an irrational construction

9

depending not so much on a national conscience as on the collective folly of the crowd, on the destructive force of exasperated instincts. It is a blind, closed nationalism, inaccessible to the concept of nation-solidarity, and not conducive to a universal humanism. This is why those African nations destined to play any historic role whatsoever will neither be Negro, Berber, or Arab nations, nor Christian, Moslem, or animist nations. They will, of course, be strongly marked by the influence of the different biological factors and by the impact of the various philosophies of their people, but above all, they will be—if they are to be anything at all—a synthesis, or let us say, a civilization. Only on this condition will they become an active element of the post-Marxian revolution of the twentieth century.

2

A POST-MARXIAN REVOLUTION

BECAUSE OF ITS OVERSEAS NATIONALISMS, the twentieth-century revolution appears as a hitherto unknown sociological phenomenon. All the great revolutions of earlier centuries, from 1789 to the Fifth French Republic, and those that have freed the rest of Europe—the last being the Soviet Revolution —present common characteristics. They all have, necessarily, an ideology inspired by classic Western humanism, emphasizing notions of liberty and the universality of man's fate. But whether bourgeois or Marxist, these revolutions bear the imprint of a dated universalism different from an integral humanism that includes all mankind.

Some will surely protest, invoking the touching generosity of the leaders of the antislavery movement, to mention only the bourgeois revolution. As for the Marxists, they will never forgive so unexpected a *rapprochement*. One must nevertheless observe that despite the superficial universality that a certain amount of pre- and post-romantic philosophy confers upon it, the Revolution of 1789, for example, remains essentially a French revolution, whatever its repercussions abroad may have been. We must not forget that the project of the federalist Cloots for a "universal republic" was rejected by the Convention after the intervention of the Dantonist Robert, who received wide support in the name of a realistic national-

11

ism, selfishly French. Fichte's views on the closed nation exerted influence on the evolution not only of European nationalism, but equally of the countries of the socialist revolution, at least during Stalin's era.

All these revolutions generally present the spectacle of a dialectical, factual opposition between the notions of "state" and "nation" as defined by territory. This opposition stems from the tension between two internal forces in perpetual hostility. Whether it be a bourgeois or a socialist regime, the problem is for the state to justify its claim that it legitimately embodies the nation; otherwise, quarrels are multiplied and conflicts break out, ending sometimes in the triumph of the one, sometimes in the victory of the other. Neither Marxist nor bourgeois revolutions escape this classic duel, and the appearance of new concepts, such as the dictatorship of the proletariat, does not alter this fundamental principle. Bourgeois or socialist, the democracies created by these historic crises have no other national basis than the traditionally decisive elements: geographical area, cultural unity, and especially the zone of historical influence. Marxism-Leninism, despite all the resources of dialectics, has made no innovations in this respect. In the final analysis, it has built the Soviet state and the new socialist nation on no bases other than those of the classical theory, formulated in different language. It is interesting that though the slogans change, the borders of the national territory strangely coincide with those of the Czarist Empire. Evidently, the revolution has not rejected all aspects of the old Greater Russia.

On the other hand, in the politically dominated countries of Africa or Asia, we are facing a new type of revolution. It is no longer a matter of applying Platonic or Hegelian ideology. If it is a question of freedom, this must be stripped of its metaphysical content, inherited from a current of romanticism. Changing the focus, freedom will be applied less to the individual than to subjected collectivities. A nation-state establishes its dominion over foreign territories, which, however retarded their technical development may be, still contain nations or homelands, even when captive. Whatever art may be deployed to prolong their slumber, before long these nations become conscious of their condition. We then begin to question the relationship between one people and another, between the dominating nation-state and the dominated nation or homeland. Because of historical circumstances that have made colonial imperialism an affair between one continent and another, between one civilization and another, the conflict in human relations does not lack racial implications at the outset and for a long time. But it is the consciousness of economic inequality that gives birth to a proletarian national sentiment, aligning the nations of Africa and Asia on the same battlefront against the West. With the consciousness of underdevelopment, a new idea appears, that of proletarian nations grouped "on the lifeline of imperialism" confronting rich nations with a geographical unity that widens the gap between them. Here, evidently, is the most original feature of the twentieth-century revolution. And this also underlines the importance of the stakes on which the peace of the world depends.

MARXISM AND COLONIAL REVOLUTION

There is no doubt that Marxism has played and continues to play an ideological role in the development of colonial nationalisms. It is crucial to determine the extent of this

13

influence. Its intervention is relatively recent. Marx was much less preoccupied with "colonies" than with the struggle of the European proletariat. His subtle, conditional support was reserved for nationalist movements likely to advance the proletarian worker movement. After the death of Marx, Engels directed his attention to the colonial question, when confronted by events in India and China. But it must be said that he was interested only incidentally in movements for colonial liberation and considered them as an aid to the forces of the world proletariat. This was in perfect accord with the *Communist Manifesto,* which recognizes no true revolution except that of the proletariat. When Lenin, viewing the growth of imperialism, had to tackle the colonial question more closely, he was led to link it more intimately with the national question. Though he contributed to the progress of dialectical analysis, he remained faithful to the main trend of Marx's thinking by subordinating the fate of nationalism to that of the socialist revolution. Self-determination of peoples was strongly affirmed and national autonomy supported as valid dialectic, politically defendable, provided that they did not imperil the victory of the proletariat. It remained for Joseph Stalin to fix these positions in the now famous article on "Marxism and the National Question." Yet even the Third International, despite the new context, despite the importance of the colonial liberation movement, did not constitute a decisive advance over the theses of classical Marxism. We know, in fact, that at the final session, Trotsky caused the adoption of "The Manifesto of the Communist International to All the Proletariat of the World," whereas it was primarily a question of the European proletarian movement, except for a brief mention of the proletariat of back-ward countries.

What we should point out particularly to the apologists of Marxism-Leninism, who pose at the same time as champions of African nationalism, is that their ideological support of the liberation movement is in reality motivated by tactical and strategic considerations. As a matter of fact, in Marxism-Leninism there could be no absolute right to independence. It could not be invoked as an abstract right, philosophically established, unconditional, as some would have us believe, an unrestricted right superseding every other. Stalin's regime offers tragic examples—notably in the republics of Central Asia—of the practical application of this concept of national autonomy. One of our best Islamic scholars, Professor Monteil, forcefully shows, in a recent volume, *Les Musulmans soviétiques,* the heavy tribute that local nationalisms had to pay for citizenship in the Soviet community. Even more serious is the fact that supporters of Marxism-Leninism tend increasingly to treat the national question as a means of serving a strategy of ideological expansion, a new opium as injurious as those that they allegedly combat. If orthodoxy forbids the attribution of equal significance to the national vocation and the proletarian vocation, to the fatherland and the social state, to the nation and the revolution, strategic interests justify the substitution, if need be, of the racial struggle for the class struggle, and the evolution of the fight against inequalities into a fight for equality.

By this subterfuge, Marxist-Leninist propaganda introduces a new mystification, a source of serious disillusionment and hatred, and arouses false hopes that young nations must guard against. Nothing is less certain than that the solution of the

15

future, the equilibrium of the world, lies in the realization of economic, social, and cultural equality. The works on paleontology produced by a mind as original as that of Teilhard de Chardin suggest, on the contrary, that the evolution of humanity seems to be headed less toward equality than toward complementarity. One has only to consider the development of the different rival economies and the relative condition of the techniques at their disposal to become convinced that the solution of the conflict between the *Tiers-Monde* and the rich world lies neither in a leveling process nor in open or secret competition based on hatred, but rather in frank and loyal co-operation, assuring mutual harmonious development.

UNDERDEVELOPMENT AND THE NOTION OF THE *Tiers-Monde*

The influence of Marxist theories on the affirmation of nationalism in the dominated countries, though far from negligible, must not be exaggerated. There is even cause to anticipate, once the young nations have acquired political independence from their former Metropoles, a new period of struggle between nationalism and foreign ideology, and more specifically, between emergent national economies and evolved economies of the capitalist or socialist types. As we shall see later, this is not an empty hypothesis. There is conclusive evidence in the Chinese revolution, despite the discretion of Mao Tse-tung with regard to Marxist orthodoxy, and in the more openly aggressive revolutions of Yugoslavia, Poland, and Hungary.

Neither the spectacular attentions of the people's democracies nor the financial, economic, and cultural assistance lavished on young African nations could prevent the outbreak of conflict between protector and protégé. One of the greatest

Africanists of the University of Moscow has just opened fire with a much-discussed study of nationalism, but his work remains on an academic level and does not disturb our neo-nationalists. Doubtless, if they are to have any real national existence, African nations will not accept second-class nationhood. They will, instead, throw off the tutelage of all competing dialectics, of every paternalism old or new, to affirm their own vocation, which basically is that of realizing a new world, a new humanity, by realizing themselves according to a new pattern. Some will probably describe this as proud pretense or extremism. We are convinced that it is on this condition that African nations will justify their birth.

For what would be the use of creating new nations, only to remain enslaved to one or another established ideology; to renounce, upon liberation, the right to liberty; or, instead of being an instrument for building an interdependent civilization, we accept a cowardly, servile role? To be a nation—and the examples of heterogeneous nations prove it—is much less to possess a past, a history, than to obtain a means of existing, of evincing a potential of incessant creativity—perpetual, unfinished, original. Like every movement against the established order, the process of forming twentieth-century nations, and therefore African nations, upsets our usual system of reasoning, challenges rules generally admitted by all, including those of Marxism-Leninism. Unless there is an ideological revision on the national question, the present alliances against capitalist imperialism will give way, in time, to merciless struggles between young nations and Communist imperialism.

Much less than Marxism-Leninism, it is, as we have said, the consciousness of solidarity in poverty, the weakness of the

17

standard of living, the inadequacy of the public services, the presence of all the elements characteristic of underdevelopment, that provide the most solid foundation for the new proletariat, officially constituted as the *Tiers-Monde* since the Bandung Conference. It is not inappropriate to recall certain geopolitical principles in order to grasp the significance of this event.

Because of the precision that economic analysis requires, some may challenge the notion of underdevelopment and prefer instead other formulas more in line with our developmental prospects. Some may discuss the criteria and dispute their applicability when trying to assign distinctive features to given economies. The favorite pastime of modern economists is to play this game, which doubtless lacks neither intellectual charm nor pedagogical interest. Nevertheless, reality is much simpler, and economists are forced to consider it. From Bastiat's theory of "economic harmonies," one must return to ideas closer to reality and recognize, in accordance with the teachings of geopolitics, a theory of "disharmony" in a world divided into unevenly developed economic zones. First of all, there are technically advanced countries, those with a per capita income of between $500 and $1,000, comprising some 500 million persons, especially the citizens of a great country called the United States of America. Secondly, there are highly industrialized countries, such as Soviet Russia, Japan, two or three European republics, and two or three South American republics, totaling 900 million inhabitants out of a world population of more than 2.5 billion, with an average per capita income of between $400 and $500. The rest, a mass of 1.5 billion, enjoying an average income of less than $100, is concentrated in two continents, Asia and Africa, structurally constituted in centers of poverty. On this specific point, Marx's theory, as revised by Lenin, has never found better support, whereas the development of capitalism in European countries has rather contradicted it.

Of the earth's inhabitants, 50 per cent do not get the minimum of calories physiologically necessary; 25 per cent lack proteins; 75 per cent are undernourished. In the first group of privileged countries, the mortality rate is 10 per cent and the life expectancy from sixty to seventy years. In the second group, comprising Latin America and a few African and Asian countries, the mortality rate is between 10 and 20 per cent, the life expectancy from forty to sixty years. And finally, in the third group, which includes the greater part of Africa and Asia, the mortality rates vary between 25 and 30 per cent, with a life expectancy of thirty to thirty-five years—the life expectancy in European countries at the beginning of the nineteenth century. Thus "the geography of hunger is also the geography of death."[1] One is amazed that in this century, when men talk so much about social justice and boast so lyrically about the progress of universal solidarity, one-sixth of the global population, composed primarily of white people, possesses 80 per cent of the total income. This fact alone is eloquent enough and excuses us, we think, from multiplying the statistical comparisons that abound in this area and that stress the great disparity in the living standards of men on our planet, at the very moment when, paradoxically, science is rushing out to conquer other planets. How has humanity reached such a degree of imbalance?

First, we must note the disparity in demographic growth

[1] Gabriel Ardant, *Le Monde en friche* (Paris: Presses Universitaires de France, 1960), p. 3.

19

from one continent to another, attributable to factors related to development. Thus swarming Asia alone contains half the world's population. This provides a basis of distribution that weakens, to some extent, the conclusions to be drawn from a comparison of national income. There is also a disparity in technical development that, far from narrowing the gaps, has merely widened them. Finally, and most important, there is a process of pauperization of the *Tiers-Monde* that has developed in the wake of colonial imperialism, under the pressure of the old capitalism. In its greed for profit, capitalism failed to understand that by creating such profound imbalance, it was condemning itself, in the more or less distant future, by inciting the hatred of the exploited masses. It failed to understand that to assure survival, it was not enough to transform colonization into colonialism. Indeed, the illusion lasted a long time, explicitly supported by the facts. The colonial period had its splendor and even today, in this age of national independence, the whole question is whether or not the era of decolonization will also be that of economic emancipation. As far as the present world imbalance is concerned, the responsibilities of the capitalist market economy are so evident that the most indulgent authors no longer dispute them.

We shall limit ourselves to the problem of the evolution of the balance of trade, which, in our opinion, provides a better index to the spoliation that victimized the primary-goods-producing countries—the very countries that belong to the *Tiers-Monde*. It would be pointless to challenge United Nations statistics, which at least have the merit of existing and of being almost the sole valid approach in this area. It would be pointless to protest a priori against studies indicating unfavorable evolution of trade in underdeveloped countries.

We often stress, not without justification, the simplistic character of schemata that classify, on the one side, underdeveloped countries as producers of raw materials and, on the other side, the industrialized countries that purchase those raw materials and export manufactured products.

The truth is more complex. Actually, the industrialized countries produce two or three times more raw materials than the underdeveloped countries and exchange with one another more food commodities than the underdeveloped countries export. Primary goods, mainly agricultural commodities, occupy an important place in the exports and trade balance of Denmark, Australia, and New Zealand. Deeper analysis shows that this argument is worthless. It is necessary to consider the percentage of the population engaged in the different sectors of production. Myrdal has observed that even when it increases rapidly in industrialized countries, production of primary goods occupies a smaller and smaller proportion of the population. In Denmark, three-quarters of the exports are agricultural products, which provide employment for no more than 20 per cent of the total population. In addition, since the resources of underdeveloped countries are more concentrated on primary goods and their cash income depends especially on exporting this output, these countries are naturally more vulnerable than the others to falling prices. Finally, there is the threat of new industrial products due to the progress of the chemical industry, the expansion of which may cause the prices of basic natural products to decline and thus aggravate the deterioration of the balance of trade. Besides its repercussion on national income, this evolution is most harmful in causing import restrictions, which in turn involve curtailment of growth and disorganization of development plans. It is possible, too, that the revalorization of prices of primary goods will not be facilitated by certain factors—some economic, such as the decline in freight; others social, such as the wage level in highly industrialized countries, where the working class, as already noted, has been able to obtain an important share of the profits.

One cannot deny the discrepancy between industrial prices and prices of primary products, particularly agricultural commodities. And when one realizes that for the *Tiers-Monde* countries, production is principally a matter of agricultural output and will remain so for a long time, one can understand the anxiety of those who denounce these trade relationships as one of the permanent causes of imbalance and increasing inequities. Whatever may be said, the dominant position of the industrial countries is reinforced by the existence of monopolistic organizations not on the level of capital goods but, strangely enough, where purchases from producers of primary goods are involved.

Pierre Moussa, who may be accused of a certain tenderness, writes: "The exports of basic products by the nonindustralized areas of the world amount to about $25 billion a year; a revalorization of 14 per cent would therefore suffice to increase the annual income of the *Tiers-Monde* by $3.5 billion, the present total of all public aid to underdeveloped countries."[2] Of their own volition the industralized nations cannot bring themselves to adopt this revalorization policy, though it is dictated by justice and reason. On the contrary, the tendency of international trade is to worsen the situation by adding to the slumping prices the instability and insecurity carefully

[2] *Les Nations prolétaires* (Paris: Presses Universitaires de France, 1960), p. 20.

fostered on the markets nowadays by the rival blocs. Thus even the international competition, instead of producing a favorable effect as could be hoped, acts against the interests of the underdeveloped countries. A recent United Nations study on the world economy in 1958 reaches precisely the same conclusions:

> One of the most serious aspects of the recent recession is its effect on underdeveloped countries.
>
> The income from their imports has decreased by 7 or 8 per cent from mid-1957 to mid-1958. Added to the gradual increase in the price of industrial goods, this represents a loss of import capacity that can be estimated approximately as the equivalent of six years of loans to underdeveloped countries by the International Bank for Reconstruction and Development, on the basis of 1956–57 prices. Because they depend on their imports of basic commodities, the underdeveloped countries see their income from imports rise slowly and after considerable delay. World industrial output increased by 140 per cent between 1928 and 1955–57, but the imports of underdeveloped countries rose by only 53 per cent during the same period or, if one excludes petroleum, by 29 per cent.[3]

The authors of this study estimate the loss suffered by producer countries at more than $2 billion, both in real income and import capacity, by reason of the fluctuating prices of raw materials during the current industrial recession. One can conclude that, in general:

> . . . the long-term prospects of exports from countries producing primary goods are no more encouraging. They depend, in large measure, on increased demand from the industrial countries. Meanwhile, purchases by the same industrial

[3] *Problèmes économiques,* No. 600, June 20, 1959.

23

countries of primary goods placed on the world markets increase much less rapidly than the income and production of these countries.

Contrasting with the slackened demand [elsewhere] for imports of industrial goods, the demand for imports by most of the underdeveloped countries tends to increase more rapidly than their domestic output. In fact, in most of these countries, economic development has necessitated a considerable rise in imports, especially of consumers' goods. Granted that the revenue from their exports increases slowly, the increased imports have caused added difficulty in the balance of payments. This is the conflict that risks compromising the ability of the countries producing primary goods to attain or maintain a sufficiently high rate of economic development.[4]

The intervention of the International Monetary Fund resolves the difficulties only partially by offering a solution to the problem of balance of payments. This is but a marginal solution, which merely exerts an indirect influence on the vital question of the instability of markets for primary goods. There will be no way out as long as the mechanisms of international trade remain what they are, with industrial countries selfishly protecting their national primary goods and continuing to levy high taxes on the primary goods of underdeveloped countries that are not yet industrialized and usually producing agricultural commodities only. Nations producing raw materials, having arrived on the international scene, not only must secure aid but must be permitted to impose new rules on international trade, and to force acceptance, firmly and jointly, of a policy of revalorization of the prices obtained for their goods.

[4] *Ibid.*

The totality of these geopolitical, economic, and social considerations gives new meaning to the manifesto of the Bandung Conference nations. Numerous Western authors have understood this problem perfectly. Jacques Mallet writes in *Le Tiers-Monde:*

> The solidarity affirmed at Bandung in April, 1955, between the colored and colonized people of two continents makes that meeting a historic event of extreme importance. The Bandung manifesto had profound impact on a mass of 1.3 billion men, slightly more than half the world population, three-quarters of the population of Asia.
>
> It has also caused considerable repercussion in North Africa and Black Africa. These ardent, unstable men who cast back in Europe's teeth her ideas, like a boomerang (without always being able or willing to take her techniques)—these men motivated by mingled admiration and revolt, by anxiety over the future and nostalgia for the past, by hunger for independence and the desire for justice—are reluctant to join any bloc, and intend to profit from the advantages[5] of a situation that they know to be dangerous. Conscious of being one of the stakes, they aspire to become arbiters. Their traditions have aroused them against the West. It would be serious for them to deem the West powerless to help them in their efforts toward accelerated, harmonious economic and cultural development, in the service of the masses. Their importance and their influence are destined to grow in the future. Their choice and their evolution will perhaps determine "the sense of history." It is in this context that the relations between unequally developed countries must be considered.
>
> In the past, these have most often taken the form of relations of domination. They must be transformed more and

[5] Advantages rather well illustrated by Russo-American bidding on the Aswan Dam.—Author.

more into relations of solidarity, uniting partners equal in rights and in dignity. The profit economy, to survive, must summon the aid of the "gift economy." One cannot say whether the current evolution will soon bring us closer to this goal, which still seems distant. The resistance of habit and selfishness, the inertia of the *status quo,* will long oppose the bold steps needed.[6]

THE NEW VOCATION OF PROLETARIAN NATIONS

The nations of the *Tiers-Monde* must understand that to equal the West they themselves must "measure up"—culturally, to be sure, but also technically and economically. It will no longer suffice to denounce colonialism and imperialism or to claim rights. They must themselves make a positive contribution to decolonization. It will doubtless be a question of satisfying needs considered basic. But, as Malek Bennabi, an Algerian Moslem writer, observes, to be effective and creative, need must become spiritualized and "transformed into an imperative for action. . . . Only thus can a society become productive and therefore a dynamic element of civilization, instead of being a simple consumer. To forge their own history, our young societies, with the advent of decolonization, will have to substitute the process of production for that of consumption and, ideologically, substitute creative initiative for the satisfaction of needs."[7]

If one tries to apply these considerations to the peculiar social category that is politics, it is necessary to express oneself in terms not of needs but of means. Thus we shall be exclusively preoccupied neither with "rights" nor with "duties."

[6] G. Balandier, J. Mallet, *et al., Le Tiers-Monde* (Paris: Presses Universitaires de France, 1960).

[7] *Vocation de l'Islam* (Paris: Editions du Seuil, 1954), p. 129.

Sociological reality summons neither of these in a fundamental dialectic that forms the mainspring of history. However, one must not forget that "duty" necessarily exceeds "right" in any ascending movement, since there must be an acquired or, in economic terms, a "surplus value." It is this surplus of duty that indicates the moral and material progress of a rising society. Consequently, a national policy that speaks of a people solely in terms of its rights is a mystification, a mythology, for: ". . . it is not a question of teaching words and slogans but methods and techniques. . . . It is not a matter of chanting freedom; they know the song. In short, the point is not to teach them what they already know, but to give them an effective method of translating their talents and knowledge into concrete social form."[8]

The effort of decolonization must lead young nations to become the principal creators of their history, by preparing themselves the technical and psychological conditions for that history. Can one create those conditions by maintaining—as in most decolonized countries, under the influence of domestic or foreign pressure groups—the economic and social structures inherited from colonialism? Or by maintaining the same sources of revenue, though a certain diversification might have been possible? Or by allowing agriculture to remain stagnant, whereas modernization of the system would eliminate an important source of inertia and cause of imbalance? Or by preventing the masses from participating in the formation of a constructive economy? Can one create the necessary technical and psychological conditions by using every possible means to avert regional co-operation, as is the deliberate policy of most of the new states?

[8] *Ibid.*

27

The African Nations and World Solidarity

Many speak eloquently of African unity. Many vehemently denounce the divisions instituted by colonial authorities. But no serious, disinterested attempt is made to correct the mistake, to effect realignments inspired by a sincere desire for unity. Instead of horizontal co-operation, many prefer—by opportunism or for reasons of personal propaganda—vertical alliances established in a spirit that aggravates the old divisions by introducing the Cold War among our countries. Beyond the common exaltation, general dissatisfaction, and revolt, we should like to see an effort made to co-ordinate our economies, to synchronize the objectives of economic planning in the various countries—at least in those located in the same economic area, in the same zone of development. We claim to be free of the West, while by the fault of the leaders of African or Asian states, Western ideologies are drawing the economic map of the liberated countries, determining the general orientation of the economic structure, allocating the markets, and establishing trade policy. Never has the presence of the West been exerted so dangerously on countries so violently jealous of their sovereignty. Never has its ascendancy been so decisively effective as in this postcolonial period.

Let us admit, in defense of the officials of the decolonized countries, that the problem of protecting national autonomy is being posed today in terms much more complicated than in previous centuries. In this rocket age, it is not easy to perfect effective techniques to repel so many clever foreign attacks. But these difficulties, though formidable, do not excuse the lack of imagination that leads to the superficial implantation of economic models conceived for other nations, in different contexts; nor do they excuse the intellectual laziness that explains the welcome extended to foreign ideologies, or the absence of real determination to create by and for oneself. We shall not push our criticism so far as to denounce the balance of the actions of the *Tiers-Monde* nations since independence, as some authors have done, not without objectivity but perhaps too rashly. One cannot reasonably speak of a balance sheet when one knows that political liberation does not confer economic liberation; that the countries of the *Tiers-Monde* have structures inherent in their underdeveloped condition and that the transformation of these structures involves other responsibilities than their own; that aid from the West—instead of being real economic and technical assistance along the lines of mutual development—is often the result of a bargain wherein commercial preoccupations are mixed with strategic or even political calculations.

Nevertheless, we will not use this as a pretext for resorting to a desiccating anticolonialism that stems from sheer political infantilism. The building of a nation is not to be confused with vain agitation, nor the progress of democracy with the temptation to anarchy, nor semi-independence with fictional independence. Yet we shall not be diverted from the effort toward self-development that is incumbent upon every nation, large or small, rich or poor, and that must enable the poor nations to break vicious circles, to reduce the curbs and cumulative effects of regressive factors, to escape from the infernal cycle and create progressively and patiently the technical conditions of harmonious development. Having become conscious of their poverty, the proletarian nations will also become conscious of their responsibilities to themselves and, above all, to the masses who expect from them more substantial nourishment than that provided by slogans.

If they fail to realize their own decolonization, they will be condemned to vegetate, to transform the twentieth-century revolution—which is to liberate countries by freeing their economy—into an abortive revolution. This would betray not only the cause of more than one and a half billion people but also that of all humanity, and would compromise the chances of a new civilization, the lights of which are just beginning to glimmer.

3

AFRICAN NATIONS AND LOCAL ELITES

FOR A LONG TIME TO COME, the underdeveloped countries, liberated or not, will summon technicians from the modern world. In this area, co-operation admittedly is necessary and must be of long duration. This stems from the technical lag of underdeveloped countries, which will disqualify them from the present competition for some time, barring a revolution. But it is also related to the fact that the fiercest nationalisms admit and preach technical collaboration, generally presented as an example of sincere, unselfish co-operation without imperialistic ambitions. This feeling, though largely justified, should be qualified in view of the sometimes doubtful competence and the poorly veiled proselytism of certain technical missions.

But the need for maintaining and developing technical co-operation should not replace the effort that must spark the technical development of the young nations and place them in the orbit of the modern revolution. Unfortunately, this desire is reflected neither in the budgets of the states, nor in the priorities established for foreign-aid funds, nor in the orientation of the local elites. With all due respect to these elites, one may note that they prefer to take the easiest way out rather than to select scientific or technical vocations that do not necessarily provide access to power or assure comfortable positions. Despite the many problems arising simultaneously, the new states must attach greater importance to research in all fields, to technology, to the construction of the necessary infrastructure, to the training of indigenous elite technicians who will participate directly in the development of their country. One has a right to expect from local elites a conception of nationalism that will make the cadres accept a national discipline. The most subjective university vocations should not escape this requirement.

The responsibility for organizing the advance of the decolonized nations toward scientific and technological progress should not divert us from another duty no less vital: that of developing national culture. In the formerly colonized Arab countries where the element of cultural continuity has been preserved despite the ravages of colonialism, educational reform and, generally speaking, the policy of national education have shown unquestionable improvement. Notwithstanding a difficult linguistic and ethnic system, India is making meritorious efforts in this direction, efforts crowned with success. The states of Black Africa, born of English or French, Belgian or Portuguese colonization, occupy an infinitely weaker position in this respect, as a result of the greater "coloniability" of their traditional cultures, and of the greater vulnerability of their civilizations, which have been more severely tested. For them, this aspect of the revolution will require long patience, technical research, and clear-sighted synthesis. Let us hope that the leaders, absorbed by organizational tasks, will not separate these from cultural problems and will not postpone the latter indefinitely. Let us hope that they are themselves unanimously convinced that without culture, no state is worthy of the name; without culture, there is no economy, no technique, no science in the service of man, no nation alive and strong.

However, if this is felt by all those responsible for the administration of the young states, we shall witness the advent of an era favorable to the resurrection of the local values of civilization. We shall take care not to remain in the trajectory of closed nationalisms. Self-sufficient culture is no more valid than self-sufficient economy. Even national culture is valid only when it is an opening, a comprehension of others, a dialogue. In other words, the elaboration of our national cultures, as of our national economies, will have meaning only in the framework of building a world civilization to be shared by all men.

4

AN ANTICOLONIALIST REVOLUTION

ON THIS POINT, however, one should entertain no illusions: the proletarian nations, and particularly the emergent African nations, will refuse to rally to this common ideal, which, with the present distribution of the world's wealth, is unrealistic. As long as things remain unchanged, this is understandable. Consequently, the chief feature of the revolution of the *Tiers-Monde* nations is its anticolonialist character. This riot of hunger, poverty, and destitution is essentially a revolt against the foreigner, whose departure will presumably lead to the disappearance of these evils. All the overseas nationalisms, African or Asian, will thus be profoundly marked by colonialisms, by foreign domination, which itself secretes hatred and xenophobia. Arab nationalism is the best example, with its virulence, its aggressiveness, and its sectarianism.

The messianic movements of Black Africa, whether of Christian or Moslem inspiration, are nothing but sociological manifestations of this collective feeling of revolt against the presence, at once material and ideological, of the foreigner. As Georges Balandier points out, it is a question of a "transfer of political reactions to religious activities . . . movements channeling the protest against a certain form of economy that has upset the traditional equilibrium by introducing insecurity."[1] A reaction, in sum, against a process of social disintegration, taking the form of a determination to reconstruct a whole ethnic ensemble.

The Mouridism[2] of Ahmadou Bamba, of Senegal, has no different meaning, except that the adaptation imposed on Islam is sociological and not political to the extent that Islam is not the religion of the colonizers. It appears, therefore, that the most urgent task for overseas nationalisms is to put an end to foreign occupation, to political domination. The revolution will have as its number-one objective the breaking of the political power responsible for economic, social, and cultural dependence, the upsetting of the idols of colonialism—by negotiation if possible, by violence if need be. Its goal will be to confer the nobility of freedom regained, even if it does not bring prosperity, even if this change of moral condition is not accompanied by a transformation of our material condition. It is in this sociology of overseas nationalisms that one must seek the explanation of the irresistible force behind the demand for independence of the *Tiers-Monde* countries. In it we must also seek the key to the aversion for capitalistic experiments and the attraction of socialistic formulas.

Since colonial power imposed the domination of foreign capitalism everywhere, there is naturally, in the mind of proletarian nations, complete identification between capitalism and colonialism, between the political system and the economic system. Balandier notes, with reference to messianic movements in Black Africa, that periods of religious crises correspond to periods of economic crises; this establishes per-

---

[1] "Messianisme et nationalisme," *Cahiers de sociologie*, XIV (1953).

[2] Mouridism is the doctrine of a somewhat fanatical and unorthodox Islamic sect in Senegal.—Tr.

35

fectly the correlation between the nationalist thrust, even in religion, and the economic situation. Thus it is understandable that in rejecting colonialism, the most conscious leaders of the organized countries reject, at the same time, the capitalist system. One can understand why they prefer the socialist system and look toward socialist experiments. Unfortunately, the question is not so simple, for it seems that colonialism is able to survive any system. This, however, has not helped to diminish the increasingly pressing demand of the colonized countries for independence. Obviously, it is less a question of effective, actual independence than of the right to independence.

But this right to independence, which is a right of the state and of the people who comprise it, must be envisaged in its dynamic aspect in the context of a given state, a given nation. Every human grouping, every society, has a right to the benefit of political independence, with the understanding that to enjoy it, it will not suffice to proclaim the right but rather to guarantee to carry out the mandate, through the existence of a democratically organized state. In other words, independence risks being a fiction unless it can be effectively exercised. Furthermore, on closer inspection, independence is only an application of a "basic right," the *right of self-determination,* an inalienable right that is nothing more than the "transposition of the free will to the scale of a homogeneous group whose members want to share the same fate."[3] The exercise of this basic right leads to solutions ranging from integration pure and simple to secession; it seems to impose itself today on the conscience even of countries with imperialistic traditions.

[3] Calvez, *Revue Action Populaire,* July–August, 1959.

As a matter of fact, it is a strict right that cannot easily be withheld from colonized peoples, long denied the advantage of political independence. ". . . not denied all advantages, for they have received something from the colonizing powers, but nevertheless denied, as long as they were subjects, a benefit indispensable to the human being. Possibly colonial tutelage was, at least in principle if not in all its acts, legitimate at a certain moment in the development of these countries. This does not exclude the fact that at another moment, it is transformed into oppression engendering frustration. This frustration is what impels people, long silent, to exercise today their right of self-determination."[4] The whole question is whether the enjoyment of this right—which no one disputes any longer—will be correlative to an effective independence of the new states and a veritable advantage to the young nations.

[4] *Ibid.*

II

Independence and Neocolonialism

5

EXAMPLES OF ECONOMIC SYSTEMS

IT WOULD BE A FATAL ERROR for the nations of the *Tiers-Monde*, especially those just recovering their freedom, to think that the struggle ends with the proclamation of independence. This admittedly is an important phase of the struggle, but it is only a first step that allows us to face up to basic tasks and crucial questions, and to apply bold solutions. A number of recently liberated states have understood fully that sovereignty in this world is real only when justified technically and economically. This is true of Israel, whose creative dynamism is constructing an imposing personality in a Middle East where most of its neighbors are not friendly. This is also true of Tunisia, where the realism of the leaders and, quite simply, of the Tunisian nation is starting the country along the road to development. This is the example that we are trying to follow in Mali.[1] One cannot warn too strongly against the illusions of nominal independence that would encourage a kind of internal immobility in so far as the old structures are concerned, and a close dependence on relations with the industrialized world.

To imagine subjects for political agitation is always easy.

[1] As Mamadou Dia explains in his Epilogue, this was written prior to August 19, 1960, while Senegal and the Sudan still formed the short-lived Mali Federation—Tr.

41

We know that one of the resources of leaders struggling with domestic difficulties is to invent a foreign scapegoat. It would be a mistake to exaggerate the possibilities of this "psychological action" that has become a method of governing.

We cannot indefinitely divert the attention of the masses from their condition, and postpone sine die the moment of reckoning. We will watch especially for a radical transformation of the economic relations with developed countries, a necessary condition for real development and consequently for real independence. On this point as well, we must view the situation clearly. The task will be difficult, for in the shadow of newly acquired independence, a veritable strategy of dependence is cleverly contrived, heralding the advent of a neocolonialism.

The Soviet offensive in the underdeveloped countries, the threat of the Cold War that weighs on African states, eloquently illustrate this new evolution toward economic colonialism. It has been estimated that during the second quarter of 1957, nearly 2,300 [Soviet] technicians worked in nineteen countries for an average of a month and a half. During the same year, Soviet universities and enterprises received about 2,000 technicians from the underdeveloped countries for training. In so far as technical aid offers the possibility of ideological conquest, we must measure all the dangers, in order not to reject it, but to take the indispensable precautions. Furthermore, the countries of the East have devised a formula for aid, replacing gifts by a policy of credits, with favorable repayment terms and interest, sometimes lower than the international rate of 1.5 per cent. But it is known that this form of assistance subjects the countries that receive it to an intolerable dependence, by depriving them of their freedom to buy wherever they please, and forcing them to supply themselves from the lending countries almost exclusively.

It will be noted, moreover, that often there is a clause requiring reimbursement in capital goods, and finally, in the case of the U.S.S.R., the prices of goods delivered under contract are fixed unilaterally. The amount of this aid from the East to the underdeveloped countries has roughly equaled, until recently, the total volume of credits granted by the World Bank to more than twenty countries: about $2 billion, of which $378 million is for military aid, the balance, $1.6 billion, for economic aid. In the battle between the ruble and the dollar, the latter has triumphed, for the United States has furnished $5 billion, the Soviet Union, $1.5 billion. But the kind of assistance provided by the Eastern bloc and the emphasis on technical aid confer, indisputably, a clear propaganda advantage upon the East.

Under the pretext of positive neutralism, the temptation for the underdeveloped countries is to surrender to the highest bidder. This would mean agreeing to make development a matter for bargaining; it would mean agreeing to transform our countries into a vast arena for sordid rivalries and to expose them to tragic consequences, at the very moment when they thought themselves free. Positive neutralism, truly neutral and really positive, ought to adopt as its policy a real independence with regard to the new strategies of domination, by requiring from the opposing blocs respect for the free development of emergent nations, and a radical revision of economic and, especially, of commercial relations, on a truly co-operative basis.

That the risks of economic neocolonialism, successor to classical imperialism, are clearly evident in this era of proclaimed independence we shall easily demonstrate, by examining as rapidly as possible several cases typical of the various systems: the economies of the Eastern Europe, those of the Middle East, and the most characteristic African experiments —those of Tunisia and Morocco.

6

THE EXAMPLE OF THE ECONOMIES
OF EASTERN EUROPE

THE MOST STRIKING EXAMPLE is provided for us by the countries of the socialist bloc, the affiliated countries of the East—the people's democracies. There is no question here of disparaging, because of our own preferences, political regimes whose accomplishments in various fields justify the favor that they enjoy with many millions of people. It is not our intention to open or reopen a debate, but to proceed to a critical examination of the facts, in so far as these can be deduced from official statistics. Let us set aside the question of whether happiness lies to the East or to the West, whether freedom is better assured here or there. The day when passions are silenced to allow an objective comparison between ideologies and systems; the day when it will be possible to make a rigorously scientific, impartial critique of the opposing experiments —on that day, the nations of the earth, which are the parties principally concerned, will reach a unanimous judgment in which even philosophers and theorists of social systems will concur.

Our role is more modest. It is to weigh objectively—quantitatively, I might say—the economic measure of proclaimed independence, first in the part of the world that boasts of having abolished imperialism and capitalism; where, theoreti-

45

cally at least, in the framework of officially recognized national sovereignties there is scarcely room for anything but socialist construction according to the principles of Marxism-Leninism.

We cannot deny, on the pretext of not accepting propaganda that does not need our support, the positive aspects of the socialist revolution, the appreciable forward strides that it has stimulated in the population of countries that have resorted to it; the economic progress that it has rendered possible, in record time, by rapid modernization of production techniques. We cannot ignore the prodigious results in the field of industrial development, particularly in heavy industry, which still remains a symbol of economic power despite the interest aroused by the progress of nuclear technique.

Having said that, let us examine the situation more closely: first of all, the general developmental conditions of this economy, the laws they obey, the norms to which they are subjected. It is necessary to note immediately that, as in colonial or semicolonial countries, the entire economy of Eastern Europe is founded on the doctrine of the territorial state and on Stalin's notion of the historical nation-community. It is a question of promoting, not great ensembles according to the socialist vision of great areas, but distinct national economies by a powerful effort of industrialization, with heavy industry enjoying the priority. What is new here by comparison with classic colonialist methods is the theory of the development of the infrastructure by heavy industry, which elsewhere remains the adjunct of the dominant economies. But this is merely an illusory progress. The implantation of production centers is not a function of the real interests of the economies concerned but of the needs of the dominant economy, that is, of the Soviet economy. Outside of Czechoslovakia and East Germany, no country of Eastern Europe presents economic conditions favorable to the creation of those coal and steel centers with which they are so "generously" endowed. On the contrary, what characterizes these regions is the scarcity of iron and the weakness of agricultural markets.

Instead of working for the environment, or even for a market of their choice, the admirable factories that are readily presented as national promotions, in contrast to the light industries of colonial territories, really function in the manner of "transformation workshops" in a market economy. Thus we detect a particularly striking paradox in the socialist economy: the dominant economy makes its partners dependent upon it for provision of food commodities, though their vocation is agricultural, and for raw materials that it must procure for them, just as capitalist French economy provides its wheat to keep the West African mills turning. This establishes a series of dependences that may be called structural, in economic terms, but that seem to us no more admissible than political dependence.

How, in short, despite the mystique of heavy industry, can we overlook the many restrictions imposed on the harmonious development of these economies? The rules of bilateralism in trade are rigorously applied, as are those of the balance of payments, calculated not in the interest of the general equilibrium of the group, but separately, nation by nation. One will observe the dramatic analogy with capitalist countries' rules of trade, the similar situation resulting from relations between Western countries and underdeveloped economies. Characteristically, the Russian doctrine, employed in dealings with the people's democracies, is precisely the bi-

47

lateralism that is the golden rule of capitalist international trade.

"As a rule," says François Perroux, "a country cannot utilize a bilateral surplus to pay its debt to a third country." The surplus from foreign trade cannot be employed between partners of the same zone, not even in the form of revisable contracts. No organ exists to co-ordinate foreign trade for the economic group. This removes any real guarantee of independence for the countries of the bloc, which have no more freedom to maneuver in foreign trade than do the dependent countries of West Africa. It is true that this bilateralism is slightly—but only slightly—corrected by triangular exchanges within the zone and by the transferability in sterling of a part of the accounts affected to some of the transactions. It is quite inaccurate to claim that bilateralism protects the economies involved against foreign imperialism and assures the development of national economies in conformity with the plan. The monetary manipulations in Poland in 1950, in Romania in 1952, and in Czechoslovakia in 1953 indicate clearly that "bilateral coupling" is not a sufficient barrier against financial perturbations. As for growth, it can really be assured only by equilibrium between "the duty to produce" and "the duty to export."

As a matter of fact, it is not enough to produce massively, or even to produce according to the most modern technical methods. One must produce according to the real needs of the economy, if it is to be superior to the colonial economy; one must be master of the sale of this output; one must be able to reduce inequalities and dependence.

In good socialist logic, one ought, on the contrary, to be oriented toward solutions of economic integration, ranging

48

from "association or co-operation of all the socialist countries"
—with free consultation within an organism of co-ordination—
to a system of close co-operation, availing oneself at the same
time "of great complexes formed by several nations" and of
links between Russia and the other partners. In reality, Soviet
Russia, as a dominant economy, cannot, in her own interest,
accept such solutions. François Perroux shows us the underlying reason for this refusal of economic federalism, which
should, moreover, be the logical consequence of socialism:

> The powers and dominant economies accept the federations
> they control and reject the federations that inconvenience
> them. During the nineteenth century, Great Britain dis-
> couraged the federalism of South American nations. After
> the World War, Great Britain, Italy, and France, firmly re-
> solved to prevent *Mitteleuropa,* had their policies of con-
> quest or control of the poles of development eventually
> supported by a Tardieu plan or a Stresa plan.
>
> Soviet Russia has maintained a network of bilateral rela-
> tions with her partners, and has tolerated bilateral agree-
> ments between her partners because, finding it advantageous
> to form and enlarge her own bloc, she could not accept the
> formation or enlargement of any other. A doctrinal reason
> sustains this option: the loud rejection of a mercantile
> economy and an international money standard. This guaran-
> tees the home country appreciable advantages within the
> socialist camp. The Eastern European partners have no gold
> or currency reserves. Russia has gold and some freedom to
> maneuver in the disposal of her surpluses, whether these
> be temporary or not. To encourage socialist nationalisms . . .
> is to isolate socialist nations from each other and prevent,
> in the absence of a medium of international exchange, any
> triangular or multilateral trade, of whatever importance, be-
> tween them. It is also to engage them in procedures of ex-

ternal trade subject to plans in which Russia has had long experience. The surest barometer here is the evolution of the foreign commerce of these countries, an examination of which reveals that while Soviet Russia's quadrupled from 1937 to 1952, that of Czechoslovakia, of Poland, of Romania and Bulgaria doubled, whereas Hungary's rose by only 50 per cent. In 1954, East Germany had 27 per cent of the intrabloc trade, Czechoslovakia 23 per cent, Poland 21 per cent, while Hungary, Romania, and Bulgaria lagged far behind with decreasing percentages respectively of 13 per cent, 9.4 per cent, and 6.5 per cent.[1]

These figures stress the increased preponderance of Russian economy and the growing disparity within the zone, with the appearance of second-zone economies. Throughout this entire period of a dependence no less onerous than political dependence, Russia has literally reigned as master, appropriating the key products; diverting trade to her own account; controlling the poles of development, the financial levers, thanks to a clever policy of "socialist participation," utilizing credits from war reparations; and—imitating her capitalist rivals—reconstituting her economy at the expense of the normal growth of the other economies. Undoubtedly, if one considers only the development of national infrastructures, this policy is effective as compared with the results obtained during the same period by the groping half measures of the dominant capitalist economies in their own spheres of interest. But, in line with Marxist theory itself, we can say neither that this progress has automatically influenced the superstructures nor that it has lessened the disparities. The per capita gross na-

[1] "Economie de l'Est," *Revue de politique étrangère,* No. 3 (1957). See also Perroux's *La Coexistence pacifique* (3 vols.; Paris: Presses Universitaires de France, 1958).

tional product, which in 1938 was 50 per cent below the level of Western European countries in such people's democracies as Bulgaria, Czechoslovakia, Hungary, Romania, and Poland, was still less in 1950, despite the increase in the rate of industrial production.

By principally stressing heavy industry, massive industrialization tends to depress the standard of living and to lower real wages by forcing an increase in importation of equipment and machines at the expense of imports of agricultural commodities and consumer goods, however vital they may be. Thus the realities of the foreign trade of the Soviet bloc reveal that structural inequalities and dependence are far from corrected, and that the theory of "capitalist encirclement" and of protection against the ravages of money economy only benefits Russia, who makes her partners pay dearly for her national self-sufficiency. By substituting barter exchanges, with profits going in but one direction, for the monetary relations of the capitalist market, the dominant Soviet economy, like any other dominant economy, reinforces its dependence on the economies it controls, and creates, finally, an untenable situation leading to ruptures, silent or explosive.

It can be affirmed that the "new type of international relations" of which the Soviet *Manual of Economics* boasts, surely does not apply the law of "mutual development" to the socialist camp. Holding all the economic levers, Russia disposes as she pleases of foreign balances, and she knows how to employ them—often in Draconian fashion—with respect to her weak partners, over whom she brandishes the threat of severe sanctions, e.g., stopping trade for lack of balance of payment. The special medium-term loans are granted under conditions particularly favorable to the Russian economy. The agreement with Yugoslavia in 1947 stipulated the opening of credits but exacted in return the output of the industries created. The loan to Poland in 1948 exchanged equipment for deliveries to be completed in 1950!

From 1954 on, no doubt, the practice of long-term agreements and development plans inaugurated a new policy that by lessening the pressure of the dominant economy, will soften its dependence on the economies over which it retains control. The now current usage of medium-term credits and technical assistance in the form of bilateral or multilateral accords will contribute substantially to the creation of a new climate, placing greater stress on co-operation. True enough, in these countries as in those of the capitalist camp where colonialism flourished—the same results proving the existence of the same causes—the popular consciousness and that of local leaders could no longer remain insensitive to the situation. We will not forget the vehement critique by Imre Nagy's ex-minister of mechanical industry, Istvan Kossa, who vigorously denounced the stagnation of agriculture and the decline in living standards. Nor will we forget the no less vehement declarations of Messrs. Gomulka and Oskar Lange against "the dogmatism of heavy industry," "the unco-ordinated planning, the incoherence of the system, and the wretched level of the workers' wages." These statements confirmed—before the revolts in Poland and Hungary—the existence of tensions within the coalition.

These tensions have lessened, however—not only for the good of the socialist coalition but also for the greater good of the world—and this is due to Soviet realism, which knows how to make corrections when necessary, and how to accept compromises in time. In this connection, we may refer to the passage in Premier Khrushchev's speech on February 14, 1956, to the Twentieth Congress of the Communist Party of the U.S.S.R., announcing agreements granting important long-term credits of 21 billion rubles to Eastern European countries, for either the purchase of consumer goods and equipment, the construction of factories, or the acquisition of foreign-currency reserves. The efforts to open new markets in the Middle East and Africa, and those undertaken to renew the dialogue with the West, are doubtless part of a plan to relax tensions. This plan is motivated by political preoccupations that it would be premature to analyze, and by an obvious desire to broaden the economic horizon and thus to correct certain distortions, certain imbalances that threaten the unity and future of the bloc.

Despite this attempt to reconvert and the feverish search for palliatives, the analysis of the trade structure, even during this phase of reaction against structural dependence, does not, on the whole, justify the assumption of liberation from the dominant economy. The general trade structure remains unaltered and the affiliated countries still depend largely on imports of cereals and raw materials. Poland—formerly a great exporter of cereals—East Germany, and Czechoslovakia now import large quantities of them. Eighty per cent of the cotton necessary for the textile factories of Eastern Europe came from Russia in 1954; the metallurgical industry went to the same source for two-thirds of its needs. It is true that the zone exports to Russia more and more of its manufactured products and equipment. There, incidentally, is a result that we would be happy to observe in colonial-type economies.

What we must remember from this analysis—we who are socialists—is that neither capitalism nor socialism automatically settles the problem of dependence, or the inequalities, economic imbalance, and tensions resulting therefrom. The socialist solution of economies coupled territorially—with national plans scrupulously separated and unco-ordinated, production centers geographically localized and not functionally organized—can stimulate prodigious technical progress. In any event, with its long-term loans for the creation of new markets, it can transform colonial-type dependence into structural dependence. But the latter cannot survive in a world that aspires to real coexistence and therefore to the elimination of all forms of domination. It is easier to try to divert attention from these inadequacies and vices, to belabor colonialism and Western imperialism. This leaves the problem untouched. Does imperialism cease to be an evil and suddenly become acceptable because one has transferred from the capitalist to the socialist camp?

We may form whatever coalitions we please; we may appeal to the most highly perfected techniques; we may make important investments and grant credit facilities, but there will be no socialist economy outside the great economic areas where harmonious development is possible.

There will be no "socialist nation" even in a regime of popular democracy, even if Marxism-Leninism is accepted by everyone—doctrinaires and men of action—without a solution of socialist integration that realizes a true interregionalization of economies and ends the hegemony of guiding nations.

The main result—whether one considers economic or social integration—is the weak degree of organic unity in the East. "A new global equilibrium for the whole has not been attained. Neither has there been formed, between 1945 and 1957, a society of nations of the socialist area, transcending national realities in the name of a social ideal, and founding a community of workers victorious over national inertias and nationalists."[2]

2 F. Perroux, *La Coexistence pacifique*, II, 248–50.

7

THE EXAMPLE OF THE MIDDLE EASTERN ECONOMIES

GEOGRAPHICALLY, HISTORICALLY, but not ideologically, the group of countries comprising the Middle East forms a specific pilot zone of development with a peculiar environment. From the economic analysis of the group one can draw useful lessons. As a basic document we shall gratefully use a volume that, in our opinion, has not yet been equaled: *Croissance économique et structures au Moyen-Orient (Economic Growth and Structures in the Middle East)*, by Professor Gannage of the University of Beirut.

Geographic unity, the existence of long-established trade routes, and racial and cultural mixing have helped to make this part of the world an old center of civilization. But the area has never been stabilized, although we find here, at least apparently, the conditions necessary for the formation of a unitary, multinational bloc, centralized or not. What first impresses us is the modern process of creating small rival nations that exist in a climate of perpetual insecurity and agitation. Nationalism in its primary form—racial, religious, mythical, sectarian—wherever it manifests itself here, is basically responsible for this evolution, against which certain Arab leaders are reacting.

This is the meaning that we attach to the action led by the

United Arab Republic and its leader, Colonel Nasser, whose ambitions and initiatives we are not obliged to share or condone *in toto.* It is always difficult to reverse the orientation imposed on history, to rectify the trend of national constructions that utilize many more emotional than rational factors. Arab nationalism, fascinated by the mirage of fractional independence, cut up and conceded bit by bit, is placed in a bad light by agreeing to wage the fight for liberation on the emotional and unrealistic level of small countries. Obviously, Western imperialism, which, long before that of Soviet Russia, proved what it could do, played on the antagonisms and rushed to the aid of different nationalist movements, following a technique in which Great Britain has far excelled France. It is curious that notwithstanding her well-known finesse and incontestable genius, France has been unable to use to advantage the opportunities that she has had, not even her undeniable cultural influence in countries with similar cultural traditions: Egypt, Syria, and Lebanon. If it be true that the disappearance of European hegemony from the Middle Eastern world makes this consideration little more than a historical reminiscence, it is no less true that new powers have stepped into the shoes of the old ones. They have taken under their august protection the same divided nationalisms, trying to rally them to their own conflicting ideologies, thus compounding domestic causes of dissension with new causes, producing disputes no less violent, no less explosive. It is in the context of these narrow nationalisms that the development of Middle Eastern economies is placed, to its misfortune, under the leadership of national sovereignties that are institutionalized and officially recognized.

Let us examine these structures to appreciate the fruits of

political liberation. The outstanding feature is that despite certain advances realized here and there—of unequal importance, depending on the country involved—we encounter on all sides unbalanced growth and unharmonious development. First, it is a brutal economy, with great disparities in the social structures comparable to those observed in colonial countries, containing large groups with an inhuman status, with extremely low levels of consumption—sometimes inferior to those of certain African colonial territories—and presenting, in addition, all the other usual criteria of underdevelopment: a high rate of population growth (2.5 per cent), and a high birth rate, particularly in Egypt. Secondly, it is a disjointed economy, with heterogeneous, unintegrated structures. Heterogeneous, because of the juxtaposition of factors that are foreign to each other, unable to make the slightest effort toward liaison or conjunction; unintegrated, because of economic atomization, a result of political divisions.

This state of affairs has grave consequences, which may be summarized. First, there is a rupture in the flow of communications between one country and the other, characterized by inadequate transport (an average of 2–3 kilometers of road per 10,000 inhabitants, the extremes being 8 kilometers for Egypt and 30 for Lebanon). It is also characterized by a lack of adequate monetary and financial institutions. This is a serious situation, which can only lead to greater dependence on foreign financial markets. The sole Middle Eastern country with an adequate infrastructure of commercial banks is Lebanon. Furthermore, structural curbs on growth are revealed by distortions in investment structure, because of the inadequate fixed social capital and its slow diffusion into agriculture; because of the existence of bottlenecks in employment; and because of barriers to investment posed by the narrow limits of national markets.

This disjointed economy is also, despite the existence of national sovereignties, a terribly dependent economy, "an integral part, a vanguard zone of Western economies." This dependence is reflected in the facts and, primarily, in the structure and role of capitalism. We have already observed that commercial capitalism really flourishes only in Lebanon, where 30 per cent of the national income comes from trade, as against 15 per cent in Israel. Furthermore, it is a capitalism tied to foreign markets and thus unable to participate in the financing of independent domestic markets. On the other hand, Israel has a reasonable amount of capital available for industry, with a rate of investment comparable to that of Western Europe. But here again it is a closed capitalism, lacking structural links with neighboring economies. Let us say that it is industrial capital of reduced effectiveness.

Predominance belongs mainly to oil capitalism. The latter, unfortunately, is too little related to domestic structures and too attached to the foreign market to be a factor of mutual development or an instrument of economic liberation and decisive progress. Investments in the exploitation of Middle Eastern petroleum are estimated at more than $2 billion in foreign capital. The importance of this figure emphasizes the determination of foreign capitalism to invest only in sectors that it deems completely profitable. Spurred by the desire for maximum profit, petroleum capitalism creates great firms in Iraq and Saudi Arabia but these firms are controlled by outsiders, imperfectly tied to their geographical territories, and tending to expand abroad. Developmental projects, programs, and plans are drawn up not as a function of the development of the Middle East or of the economies that comprise it, but in the interests of the great international oil trust.

No doubt the exploitation of petroleum, organized technically and financially to procure substantial profits for foreign capitalist enterprises, is not—far from it—without appreciable benefit for the producing countries. The increasing number of development centers as a result of numerous discoveries of rich deposits, especially in Iraq, is evidently a factor for growth by its effects on construction and the demand for complementary products and investments. These effects remain necessarily limited, however, creating zones of prosperity in the vicinity of zones of poverty, for want of rational handling of the problem of adequate communications and trade networks.

As a matter of fact, in most instances it is a question of complementary investment, centered on an industry foreign to the country where it is implanted. Such investments, Professor Gannage observes, have no influence on the Middle Eastern economy. The mechanisms of diffusion, through the secondary effects of the multiplier, are unknown in this region. Oil centers are not poles of development that inspire, by their dynamic impact, a host of complementary industries. No appreciable increase in employment ensues, except for the small number utilized in the petroleum industry. Likewise, the countries producing oil do not benefit from the higher national income that would result if the reinvested profits produced diffusion that would gradually affect the entire population.

But, by detaching themselves from Middle Eastern economies, the oil centers constitute outposts of industrialized countries and are naturally integrated into their economy.

The secondary effects of the multiplier will appear, not as they normally should, in places where the petroleum exploitations are located, but in the countries from which the investments come. This upsets the natural trend and produces an adverse effect through which weak doses of colonialism still filter.[1]

Yet it would be unfair to make oil capitalism solely responsible for the lag in growth of Middle Eastern economies. The producing countries, which receive sizable royalties—almost a billion dollars a year—do not make the best use of these funds, which, judiciously employed, would surely have contributed to the evolution of economic structures. But waste and prestige expenditures are the rule in most of these countries, especially in Saudi Arabia. In contrast are expenditures of an economic nature, particularly those that would have permitted the realization of basic investments by earmarking a part of the royalties. It is necessary to point out, however, some progress in investment; under the pressure of local nationalisms, an integration movement is beginning to stimulate "constructed growth." Even Saudi Arabia, despite its political institutions, has become conscious of this need and allocates 30 per cent of its petroleum royalties to public works: ports, airfields, railroads, power plants, waterworks. Iraq, which has championed this policy in the Middle East, has devoted 70 per cent of its oil royalties to finance its first economic plan and anticipates from these same resources a substantial contribution of about £260 million to finance the second plan, which requires a total of £488.5 million. It is true that these efforts are limited by the inadequate capacity of the economies

[1] Gannage, *Croissance économique et structures au Moyen-Orient* (Paris: Librairie de Médicis, 1958), p. 108.

of the oil-producing countries to absorb large amounts of financing. This is why the Arab states are right to lay the foundations of a Middle East oil community, the object of which is to promote the growth of this region, in the manner of the Johnston plan for the Jordan Valley.

An examination of the structure of international trade is equally indicative of the dependence of Middle Eastern economies. Despite political independence, despite the pronounced anti-Western attitude of Arab nationalism—especially anti-Western Europe—these countries are still dependent on the West in so far as foreign trade is concerned.

This dependence is evident in the structure of imports and exports, in the disparity of income, and finally, as with every underdeveloped country producing primary goods, in the variation of terms of trade. As has been noted for West African countries, the predominance of the agricultural sector—especially the fact that this agricultural output is restricted to a few basic commodities—is the principal cause of the weakness of the Middle East's trade with Europe. More than one-third of the exports from the fertile crescent formed by Egypt, Iraq, and Syria goes to the European market in the form of cotton and cereals. Egyptian cotton exports represent 80 per cent of that country's exports, while exports of Syrian cereals total 30 per cent. These figures reveal the excessive vulnerability of these economies, particularly that of Egypt, largely dependent on the European market and seriously affected by instability in demand. It is understandable that Egypt is trying to loosen the noose, by expanding her relations with the U.S.S.R. and Czechoslovakia, after the vexations caused by the American cotton policy. Statistics establish the same dependence with respect to imports. Whether it be Iraq and

Israel on the one hand, or Egypt on the other, one-third of the imports come either from the United States and Great Britain, or from Western Europe.

There is, however, a definite tendency on Egypt's part to increase her imports from the countries of Eastern Europe. This structural dependence of Middle Eastern trade on the fluctuations of the European market, and consequently of the world market, explains the instability of prices, its repercussions on the increasing disparity between incomes, and the resulting social malaise that makes this part of the world a constant hotbed of revolt. Development plans are needed, but the fluctuation of prices renders difficult, if not impossible, any plan of economic development based on a normal rate of growth. Industrialization is necessary, but the agricultural concentration and the absence of an infrastructure with a modern foundation banish this prospect. Thus one can understand why it should be Egypt, so vulnerable structurally, and so dependent, that serves as a center of revolt against the West. One can understand why she sets the tone, not only on the political plane, but also—and this is certainly more effective—on the plane of economic liberation, with a policy of liberation by adequate measures, the most crucial of which is not nationalization, but restrictions on luxury imports and manufactured goods. And finally, one can understand why, in the East-West rivalry over the oil fields, the policy called positive neutralism is something quite different from Indian neutralism, since it is in reality more favorable to the Soviet Union and the people's democracies. This tendency has been openly stated since the Suez incident, which caused the break with the "imperialist" powers of the West and marked the start of an era of technical and economic co-operation with the East in the hope of industrializing the Middle East.

Thus Egypt will finance her five-year plan thanks to an agreement with the U.S.S.R. granting matériel on credit in the amount of £62 million Egyptian, and a pact with the Federal Republic of Germany for a loan of £46 million. Thanks also to credits negotiated for with the U.S.S.R. in December, 1958, a series of projects will be realized: the creation of industries for extracting minerals, the construction of airfields, a plant for processing butter, an electric power plant in Suez, and (completed in 1959) a shipyard at Alexandria. The determination of the Egyptian government to exercise state control from now on over industrial enterprises is reflected in the creation in January, 1957, of a new organism, the Economic Organization. This agency protects the public interest in all firms in which the state has shares; it buys companies or capital stock sequestered since the Suez affair; launches projects that private concerns refuse to finance; co-ordinates activities in the private sector by subjecting all industrial expansion to prior approval and by arranging assistance for new industries.

Following this reorganization, the role of the Industrial Bank as a provider of production-goods investment was considerably reduced in 1957 but loans and advances made by the bank to industry increased appreciably during the year, reaching £2.6 million Egyptian, as against 0.7 million in 1957 and 1.8 million in 1955. The chemical and metallurgical industries, as well as the textile industry, were the main beneficiaries of the increased volume of credit.[2]

[2] "L'évolution économique du Moyen-Orient, 1957–1958," *Problèmes économiques*, February 16, 1960.

In Iraq one finds the same determination to liquidate archaic structures, to escape from the grasp of the dominant economies, by the preparation of a development plan that gives industrialization projects the place they deserve. In "Pour une industrialisation de l'Irak," Pierre Rossi paints an impressive picture of this evolution. The British experiment had resulted in a resounding failure.

The Iraqi people, already nearly dying of hunger, were no longer cultivating more than one-fifth of the arable land in 1958; agricultural output kept dropping. The production of dates, the principal food commodity in the country, declined between 1955 and 1956 from 420,000 to 250,000 tons. According to medical surveys made under FAO auspices, undernourishment was responsible for 50 per cent of the infant mortality; life expectancy was limited to about thirty years. . . . And how could it have been otherwise, since the agricultural output had declined to one of the lowest levels in the world? The income of a fellah from the provinces of Amara and Kut rarely exceeded twenty francs per day, that of a Baghdad worker 150 to 200 francs. The cities were islets of inflation where the currency, between 1950 and 1955, was devalued by 25 to 50 per cent. Income from real estate attained a rate of 30 per cent, while rent tripled between 1952 and 1958. To this stagnation was added widespread unemployment which struck at least 21 per cent of the rural population and as much as 60 per cent of the city dwellers. Illiteracy extended to 90 per cent or even to 99 per cent of the population in certain regions.

This was the nadir to which a country had been reduced, a country rich in history, in happy memories, with water, land, and raw materials, sparsely settled in proportion to its resources, and occupying in the heart of ancient empires a trade route of unquestionable importance. The extent of this degradation was brutally revealed to the Western public—

which until then had been carefully kept ignorant of the situation—by the revolution of July 14, 1958, that stirred to the depths the Iraqi masses, from Kurdistan to the Persian Gulf.

Since that date, these masses have been demanding a prompt remedy for their ills. The young teams in power, who have the perilous responsibility of restoring order, include good economists trained for the most part in European universities. To progress as fast as possible, they thought it necessary to realize the industrialization of the country before 1964, combating anarchy with a race against the clock. The Ministry of Economic Planning in Baghdad is now the center of feverish activity that makes it the hub of the entire Mesopotamian future.[3]

The crucial event was the pact of technical co-operation signed by the Baghdad government and the Soviet Union in March, 1959, for Iraqi industrialization. The mining studies snatched from the Anglo-Saxons were entrusted to Soviet experts, who received, in addition, authorization to draw up maps and master plans. The new regime resulting from the July, 1958, revolution decided to suppress the Office of Development, previously created by the Anglo-Saxons, and to replace it by a plan with the following objectives.

1. Liquidation of imperialist hegemony, the fundamental and decisive cause of the very backward economic condition;
2. Liquidation of the social interdependence resulting from the feudalism on which the imperialists leaned; and
3. Construction of an independent, progressive Iraqi economy.

[3] *Problèmes économiques* (February 2, 1960) pp. 16–17.

The effort will be concentrated principally on: the refining industry, whose modernization by Soviet experts will permit the creation of a petrol-chemical industry utilizing all the subproducts of distilling; the creation of a series of industries oriented toward agricultural development; fertilizer factories, coupled with factories for treating sulphuric acid and sulphur; and a metallurgical unit to furnish spare parts for mechanized agriculture. But to realize this vast program, which, as in every underdeveloped country, poses technical and human problems—such as those of cadres and of labor—Iraq seems unfortunately to have rejected any idea of an economic community, preferring the illusory doctrine of self-sufficient development.

Arab nationalism has driven the Westerner from the Middle East, which has been forced to admit others, to open the competition to the Soviets. The Middle East hopes, by virtue of positive neutralism, to obtain the best advantage from its new tactics. In following this path, Arab nationalism is no doubt taking grave risks. It would perhaps be wiser to integrate this policy into the general framework of the development of a coherent Middle East community, economically and technically—if not politically—attuned. Otherwise, there will be no independent Middle Eastern economy, whatever techniques may be employed; whatever the importance of its resources, in oil or other products; whatever the value of its exports; whatever the developmental strategy.

8

NORTH AFRICAN EXPERIMENTS: THE MOROCCAN AND TUNISIAN ECONOMIES

FOR OUR OWN EXPERIMENT, it should prove most instructive to glance at the evolution of the North African economy since the end of the protectorate over the Sherifian Empire and the Regency.[1] We shall examine successively the Moroccan economic situation after independence and the principal economic aspects of the new Tunisia.

BALANCE SHEET OF THE MOROCCAN EXPERIMENT

The attainment of independence has doubtless enabled Morocco to realize structural reforms on the administrative level that would have been impossible under the protectorate. One will note, among others, the communal reform, by far the most revolutionary, which will surely have a most profound influence on traditional structures and serve the new regime as the best tool for decolonization. Furthermore, it will be observed that despite a permanent social crisis and a certain internal effervescence, independent Morocco is succeeding in maintaining order, thanks to an exceptional financial

[1] The French protectorate over Morocco (Sherifian Empire), began in 1912; the protectorate over Tunisia (the Regency) began in 1881.—Tr.

effort that absorbs 25 per cent of the budget. Morocco can also take pride in having been relatively successful in gaining unquestionable prestige for its young international personality.

Perhaps it can even be reproached, not unreasonably, for manifesting this preoccupation too blatantly, like all young states. Perhaps political considerations take precedence over the imperatives of internal development and the search for solutions likely to endow the country with the institutions of a modern state. Moroccan nationalism, the basic grievance of which was quickly satisfied, does not seem to realize that the accession to independence marks the beginning of a new phase: the struggle to consolidate that independence.

An analysis of Moroccan social structures indicates that their evolution unfortunately has not kept pace with political evolution. The rural masses, representing 70 per cent of the population, "are not in the movement," but remain marginal, participating neither directly nor indirectly in the task of national renovation. At the moment, nothing in their standard of living—food, clothing, or housing—justifies the statement that the advent of independence has been the starting point of a new era of social progress. The new urban proletariat, comprising 20 per cent of the population, is potentially a dynamic force capable of furnishing excellent cadres for economic development. It seems, unhappily, to be too hetero-geneous and, despite appearances, not sufficiently conscious or organized, and, we dare say, too addicted to politicking— which is not exclusively a Moroccan evil—to play the full role that might be expected of it. Actually, the whole weight of Moroccan economic development rests on the middle classes, especially on the economic *bourgeoisie,* the small mer-chants and government workers. This is a conservative *bour-*

69

geoisie; besides, it is small and of only average quality, insufficient to carry on the necessary revolution, much less to assure its success.

The shortage of Moroccan social institutions cannot fail to have serious effects on development in all sectors. It explains, for example, the effects of restraints on capital formation, directly related to restraints on investment, on which the margin of profit has been reduced; the effects of restraints on cultural development, a consequence of an unrealistic educational policy that fails to take into account the need for competent and sufficiently numerous teaching personnel; and finally, the effects of restraints on administrative organization, which, despite intelligent reforms, is not as efficient as it should be, because of the shortage of qualified cadres.

"The action of restraints on capital formation and on investment return is catastrophic. The example of the irrigated area of Doukkala is the best illustration of this. On the coastal plain behind Mazagan, an area that will be the second largest (247,110 acres) is being irrigated."[2]

At the moment, starting from the great Im Font Dam on the Oumer Rbia, 24,710 acres are irrigated; reorganization has been effected, the land surveyed, the secondary canals are finished, the water reaches the fields. Before irrigation, the land, planted with cereals, brought in about 40,000 francs per 2.471 acres. Today it would be possible to cultivate fodder plants, alkaloids, tobacco, and early vegetables. For five years, cotton on the experimental fields has given a "long silk" fiber of remarkable quality. In other words, the income per 2.471 acres should rise to 150,000–200,000 and even 300,000 francs. Yet, for two years, except for a few lucerne

[2] "Un nouveau pèrimétre d'irrigation: les grands travaux de la plaine des Abda-Doukkala," *Bulletin d'information du Maroc,* July, 1954.

fields, the fellah still grows barley and wheat. The total loss in national income exceeds one billion francs. Profit from the enormous investment is nonexistent. To start this area producing, one would need only a section leader familiar with irrigation problems and able to persuade the fellahs to co-operate in the use of machines, in the construction of tobacco dryers, in the commercialization of their goods, etc. One would need only an agronomist experienced in calculating schedules for plants and seasons; a team of monitors to work with the fellahs, oversee the rotation of crops, and conduct experiments. But it will take a long time to find these men.[3]

A study of the economic structures of independent Morocco confirms what the administrative superstructure and the social structure suggest: a disjointed, dominated, and concentrated economy. As in every retarded economy, one of the characteristic features is the predominance of the agricultural and mining sectors. Agriculture, which occupies 47 per cent of the active population, is unfortunately backward and adapts poorly to the necessity for modernization, primarily because of the excessive parceling of land and the rural exodus, which render any agrarian reform difficult. Since the use of authoritarian methods of collectivization is prohibited by the local mentality, the only possible formula for agricultural association is the co-operative. But the success of co-operative development requires cadres, a reconciliation to agriculture of urban elites, particularly of young people, administrators as well as accountants. Unfortunately, in independent Morocco and in Mali, the urban young people are not always willing to abandon the facilities of city life for an austere existence in the interior. Let us add that agricultural progress is also impeded

[3] R. Lenoir, "L'Economie marocaine à l'épreuve de l'indépendance," *Cahiers de l'I.S.E.A.*, Series F 12, p. 128.

by the complexity of the water problem and by the disturbing ravages of erosion, which threatens invasion by the desert.

Though an agricultural country, Morocco is also a great mineral producer. It ranks third in the world in the production of phosphates and tenth in lead; this represents a global exportation of 35 billion francs. Its potential in mineral production is limited by insufficient production of energy. Coal is rather scarce and of mediocre quality; petroleum output does not exceed 90,000 tons and that of electrical energy has reached its peak. Though the country possesses a fine network of roads, thanks to colonization, it has but one railway. This makes transport of commodities difficult and tends to retard economic growth. Adding this negative factor to the inadequacy of agricultural output and energy, one understands why industrialization cannot progress rapidly, despite the determination of those who direct the economy.

A second feature of the Moroccan economy is that after ten years of total sovereignty, it remains a disjointed, or more precisely, a "nonarticulated" economy. Whereas the traditional population lives in a closed circuit, in the framework of narrow markets, limited by the regional boundaries, the modern sector, divorced from the former, is completely allied to the capitalist European economy. It is 80 per cent European, notwithstanding the dynamism of the local *bourgeoisie* and the virulence of the trade-union movement. This nonarticulated character of the diverse sectors of the economy has grave effects on development and growth. In such an environment, the diffusion of prosperity from the modern sector can operate only imperfectly, producing little acceleration of progress in other areas. Any contraction of the capitalist sector, which has alone benefited from the prosperity, blocks the entire process of growth in the whole economy. It has no other source of vitality. Finally, in an economy so clearly dualistic, the phenomena of underinvestment and overinvestment coincide in both sectors with industries that are fully mechanized with labor-saving equipment. The best example is that of the sardine factories.

Let us note a few facts that reveal and explain the fragility of the Moroccan economy. These are, first, the decline in bank deposits, which were 132.1 billion francs in 1954, 127.3 billion in 1955, 86.7 billion in 1956, and reached 89.5 billion in 1957. Next, the balance in the general treasury dropped from 18 billion francs in 1955 to 8 billion in 1956. The building index declined by 50 per cent; quotations on real estate fell by two-thirds; there was a decline in imports of industrial vehicles and tractors; and, finally, to complete the picture, there was dramatic unemployment, affecting 20 per cent of the active population.

In addition, the Moroccan economy is more than ever a dominated and a concentrated one. The thirst for immediate profit, conforming to the old capitalist doctrine, fatally entails a concentration of investment around ports and points of exit. In Mali, we are only too familiar with its baneful effects: a rural exodus depriving the countryside of hands needed to cultivate indispensable food; a monstrous urban development with all the resulting social problems and disorganization. These are difficulties that independent Morocco has not yet resolved and will not resolve without a policy of harmonious growth and a development plan. Despite the political slogans, the structure of foreign trade indicates the dependence of Moroccan economy—a state of dependence strangely resembling that of colonial territories. "Imports," Lenoir writes, "represent between one-fourth and one-fifth of the resources, and exports, one-fifth of employment. Here again we encounter the typical structure of underdeveloped countries, with all its dangers in a period of contraction of trade or decline in prices of raw materials."[4]

In recent years, Morocco has doubtless made a serious attempt to reduce the deficit in its trade balance, by raising the proportion of exports to imports from 50 to 70 per cent, and by lowering the deficit in its balance of payments from 46 billion francs in 1955 to 30 billion in 1956. These brilliant results have been possible only as a consequence of lower purchasing power on the one hand, and of an increase in exports to the franc zone on the other. We must not forget that France's share in Morocco's foreign trade varies between 50 and 60 per cent; that French investments represent more than three-quarters of foreign investments in Morocco; that belonging to the franc zone has allowed Morocco to settle imbalances with the various monetary zones. Because of all these ties, the Moroccan economy is interdependent with the French economy.

It is appropriate to add that Morocco owes this privileged position not to a reconversion of an independent economy inspired by the brand-new theory of mutual development, but to the effective action of the French "colony," which forms an important minority there. It will be noted, moreover, that though the Moroccan government affirmed its will to independence by the monetary measures taken since October, 1959, devalued the Moroccan franc, and instituted controls on foreign exchange between Morocco and other countries

[4] *Loc. cit.*, p. 140.

of the franc zone, it nonetheless evinces a certain realism by affirming that "Morocco is advancing along its own road but recognizes the importance of its ties with France."

From all this, it follows that the Moroccan economy is severely tested by independence. What we know of the political and social situation, the reigning confusion and the violent upheaval that has just occurred among Moroccan cadres all justify an anxiety for the future that neither expansionist claims in the direction of Mauritania nor even agitation against the French atomic explosions can dissipate. We hope that Morocco will gain a clear consciousness of its problems that will place it on the road to building a progressive economy, based on rapid industrialization, training of economic and financial elites, and socialist planning of public investments.

The Tunisian Experiment

The Tunisian economy had exceptionally favorable characteristics on the eve of independence. In contrast to the evolution in Morocco, colonization, instead of perpetuating the old institutions and building a capitalistic economy in juxtaposition, had the merit of proceeding—to quote an original expression—to a veritable "creative destruction." Refuting theses that we formerly supported—under the influence of radical Marxist theories whose lack of scientific accuracy in relation to contemporary realities we have since discovered—we must admit that in the specific case of Tunisia, the French protectorate played a role of collective economic creation, according to the concept defined by François Perroux in his General Theory of Economic Progress. It is easy to cite facts of growth and development, indices of its progress.

To begin with, there is the evolution of rates of growth of the Tunisian and European populations, the former rising from 0.5 per cent between 1921 and 1926 to 1.6 per cent between 1926 and 1936, and subsequently to 2 per cent. The rate of growth of the European population fell from 5 per cent between 1881 and 1921 to 2 per cent between 1921 and 1936, and then to 1 per cent. Traditional commodities have also shown growth: cultivation of cereals, the olive-oil industry, fishing, fruits; new products: viticulture, extraction of minerals, industrial goods; a greater volume of foreign trade, with rates on the order of 4.2 to 3.6 per cent. There has been, in short, a massive increase in economic indicators of progress. One may wonder whether this has been accompanied by a transformation of economic structure. As Zarka observes:

> The absence or the poor quality of long series of statistics unfortunately prevents definite analysis of structural modifications in the Tunisian economy.
>
> One should note, however, the increasing proportion of the industrial sector during 1935–45, and the intense commercial activity in urban centers since the end of World War I. Also noteworthy is the added importance of railway, road, maritime, and air transport, in relation to the rapid increase in mining, the commercialization of local products, and the increase in exports and imports. As a consequence, the share of agriculture has certainly declined, despite the enormous quantitative increase of each of the agricultural activities.[5]

We may therefore conclude that there has been a change of structures, perhaps better interpreted as an interpenetra-

[5] *Cahiers de l'I.S.E.A.*, Series F 12, p. 165.

tion of the traditional economy with the modern, which is a progressive extension of modern capitalist economy, due to a distribution network created by colonization, and also to "the effect of imitating European models." A process is thus established that subjects a more and more sizable mass of Tunisians to the discipline of the monetary market. It is estimated that because of this accelerated diffusion of progress, a million and a half Tunisians have acquired the socioeconomic reflexes of the capitalist sector, and that this sector now includes almost one-half of the population. We shall not elaborate on other indices of progress, such as the increased per capita output, the per capita increase in revenue, the rise in per capita consumption, the evolution of the structure of income distribution, the increasing number of wage earners, or the population growth of 65 per cent in thirty years.

As we know from experience, all these favorable indices do not justify the conclusion that the economic development necessarily denotes the well-being of the local population and the advancement of the Tunisian economy. We also know that despite this economic progress, underdevelopment persists in some sectors, with Moslem workers suffering from being uprooted, from unemployment, and from the growing disparity between actual and desired consumption. It is, moreover, important to note that the collective creation following the creative destruction has not resulted from individual initiative, but from the colonial state and sometimes from oligopolistic groups. It is the state, not private initiative, that has provided the incentive and economic infrastructure, has adapted the institutional cadre to development, and has stimulated the private capitalist sector, which in turn has stimulated the purely Tunisian sector, thus allowing a local *bourgeoisie* to emerge. Thus Tunisian economy contrasts enormously with colonial-type economies, and this privileged situation underlines still more the difficulties that confront independent Tunisia.

The problem will be to maintain the patrimony inherited from the protectorate, to retain the momentum in order to speed up growth and development. This will not be easy, for the factors are rather unfavorable when one examines the situation immediately following independence. But the basic question, which must dominate the policy of the leaders of the Tunisian state, is to place the development thus far achieved at the service of the new nation, to entrust the key sectors to the state or its nationals, to proceed with institutional and, especially, agrarian reforms that will guarantee the restoration to the local peasantry of the best lands, which were seized by foreign settlers. In a word, the basic question is to make this economy, which has structurally passed the typical colonial stage, a national Tunisian economy.

Fortunately, the National Congress of Tunisian Workers, which willingly agreed to silence its grievances to support the program for economic progress, has become conscious of these necessities. The trade-unionists of Mali will probably read with interest the economic report enthusiastically approved by the Congress. It is true that things will not always work so smoothly, and that Tunisia, like Mali, will have her trade-union crises, and for reasons curiously similar. But Tunisia's well-balanced nation has been able to advance along a middle road that assures stability. She has understood that political problems do not solve problems of growth, increased productivity, and a higher living standard for the toiling masses. Tunisia knows that one of her first objectives must be rapidly

78

to overcome the internal imbalance—by developing the hitherto neglected central and southern areas, by an effort toward industrialization emphasizing increased production of electrical energy, by the rapid training of cadres facilitated by an intelligent reform of education, and, finally, by a wise policy of mutual exchanges and co-operation. This would no doubt have been especially fruitful with her old friend France, if the Algerian question had not arisen to spoil relations and seriously preoccupy all Tunisia.

The national upsurge that engages Tunisia in the economic battle is all the more necessary because the country's difficulties are not negligible. Obviously, the economic situation was not particularly flourishing immediately after independence. This is corroborated by the author Préjean, a member of the Tunisian Communist Party: "To the extent that the new Tunisia has not torn herself away from the paths of traditional capitalism, various indices of economic lag could be detected after the proclamation of independence. This decline could have become much more serious if Tunisia had not been fortunate enough to enjoy a series of good agricultural years after 1955–56."[6] And the author goes on to list successively the significant slump in bank deposits during this period, the drop in savings deposits and postal accounts, and the reduction of private investments as a result of the departure of many Europeans. Furthermore, he mentions the contraction of the economic sectors, except mining and oil (controlled by the trusts), the failure of firms, and the important reduction in capital. Gold imports declined from 3,300 pounds in the years 1952 and 1956 to less than 2,000 pounds

[6] "L'Economie tunisienne depuis l'indépendance," *Economie et politique,* June, 1959.

79

in 1956, and then to less than 550 pounds in 1957. The same phenomenon was observed in the stock market quotations.

This economic slump was also detected by an author noted for his Tunisian sympathies, Destanne de Bernis:

> A crisis of confidence surely accompanied independence. It was reflected in a trend toward recession in ⸝conomic activity, by the slackening private investments, but also and most important, by a particularly disturbing hemorrhage of capital. The Europeans took their capital back home, and not only those who returned to the Continent; the Tunisian *bourgeoisie* did not hesitate to transfer its funds in the same direction, while industrialists took advantage of rediscounts from the Bank of Algeria and Tunisia to borrow on short term and transfer money to France, in the form of industrial working capital, which could be utilized in case of an eventual withdrawal. This was a special form of disguised disinvestment, not without influence on the country's economy, in addition to being a sword of Damocles. One cannot overemphasize how much the delay in controlling transfers—not to mention blocking them—cost Tunisia. This control was not exerted until January, 1959, after French devaluation. The difficulties confronting Morocco in June–July, 1959, were even greater because it delayed even longer. Without disputing the troubles imposed by any system of control, its effectiveness was demonstrated by the constant increase of cash reserves in the Central Bank of Tunisia since December 31, 1958. Whereas they had declined dangerously until that time, they rose from 19.8 million dinars at that date to 27 on May 29 and to 31.6 by July 31. This was the first time in history that the value of Tunisian crops remained available for the economic development of the country.[7]

[7] *Revue de l'action populaire*, January, 1960, pp. 35–36.

The Tunisian budget could not be balanced because of the crushing burden resulting from the expenses of independence and the increased administrative requirements of the state. As a matter of fact, the budget rose from 60 to 80 billion dinars without benefiting the productive or social sectors. The budgeted expenditure could not be achieved except by loans or indirect taxes that raised the cost of living. These taxes accounted for 50 of the 60 billion anticipated from collections; the rest was provided by foreign loans and aid (especially French).

Tunisian commerce remained tied to France. Until 1958, Tunisian exports to France reached 62 per cent, while imports from the same country totaled 71 per cent. Tunisia was able to adjust her trade balance for the first time in years, but this was due to exceptional harvests of cereals that enabled her to increase exports and reduce imports.

It is therefore understandable that Tunisian leaders are launching a campaign for economic independence. It is to be hoped that this is not a mere political slogan, and that it means something more than a simple rupture with the franc zone, a rupture crowned by unpegging the dinar. It is to be hoped that the Tunisian government, which has already adopted constructive policies, especially in agriculture (with the creation of a Development Fund for the Center and South, a pilot project in the same regions, a management plan for Cape Bon, etc.), will hasten to break with a certain empiricism inherited from the protectorate and will adopt an economic doctrine and a development plan in line with this doctrine. In fact, we are tempted to believe that:

> . . . the economic bases chosen by the national *bourgeoisie* in power are still uncertain. The present overvaluation of the

dinar causes increasing difficulties for Tunisian exporters on the French market, and we know how vital this market is for Tunisian foreign trade. The rupture of Franco-Tunisian financial relations forces the Tunisian *bourgeoisie* to turn to other lenders and sources of investment. The future of any development program supported by classical capitalist methods—which this *bourgeoisie* does not reject—and the future of any free enterprise that appeals to foreign investors, are compromised by measures intended to protect Tunisian producers, to prevent the flight of profits, to give Tunisians management or control of all national resources. Thus it is a contradictory policy, which ends with concessions to capital similar to methods at least a century old.[8]

Perhaps these criticisms would be more valid if they were less categorical. Nevertheless, the Tunisian economy remains on the whole too dependent on this influence of classical liberalism. The result is that despite some praiseworthy initiatives, they are still at the stage of old-style appeals for capital. These formulas are tantamount to a rejection of all hope for socialization. Budgetary techniques are still centered on the sacrosanct notion of the balanced budget, even if it means concealing more serious imbalance. This is why, instead of adopting a policy of growth—which would have hastened the preparation of the long-awaited plan to start Tunisia on the road to development—they have kept a mercantile perspective. They have been anxious primarily to market their goods, sometimes at considerable loss because of the purchase of secondary and luxury commodities from buyer countries. For the success of the Tunisian experiment, we hope that after a long period of groping—perhaps necessary and certainly understandable—an economic policy will finally be determined.

[8] Préjean, *loc. cit.,* p. 63.

A FEW CONCLUSIONS

From examples as diversified as those just reviewed, we can draw certain conclusions that will benefit our own experiment and help us to see more clearly, now that we, in our turn, are about to undergo the hard test of independence. No one denies that independence is a legitimate aspiration, not even those who used to dispute it to safeguard their interests. But more than a legitimate aspiration, more than a right, independence is a duty for any country under foreign domination: the duty to affirm its vocation as a state, to participate actively, sovereignly, and fully in world progress. The universal creative undertaking to which we are invited by socialist or Christian progressives cannot be conceived, much less realized, in a world where slave nations still exist, with people deprived of the normal exercise of their national vocation.

Independence is therefore not only an obligation for nations that have yet to liberate themselves, but also a duty no less forcefully imposed on all humanity, for which it tends to be something new: a collective vocation. More concretely, independence appears as a major advantage, if not a precondition, for helping to achieve national development. We need not stop to list its virtues. Its psychological merits, with all the potential of energy that they imply, are not the least important. We prefer to stress the dangers of an attitude of euphoria that tends to make one accept a means as an end, thus paving the way for a rude awakening. We must not forget that independence is a means, a potent means, to enable proletarian nations to assure their rapid development by integrating modern economies into a world economy on the basis of equitable co-operation.

Let us add immediately that no development will confer real independence from powerful economies—socialist or capitalist—that tend to strengthen their domination, unless we can achieve vast communities transcending traditional territorial limits, reversing habits of thought and destroying old myths that narrow nationalisms try to preserve. The economies of the Middle East, of the people's democracies in the East, and of North Africa would enjoy greater progress if their development could be assured in larger groupings.

This lesson is valid for West African economies, which are perhaps exposed to even greater risks because of the Balkanized condition in which they are attaining independence. The new market that they form, at a time when East-West rivalry is so keen, makes them easy prey for a new kind of colonization. It is vain to hope that positive neutralism will assure the development of African economies. The Indian example would be misleading because India practices neutralism within an organized whole. On the contrary, the example of the neutralist policies of the Middle East, which lack the support of a coherent economic ensemble, must make us reflect upon the consequences of an attitude that may prove to be more disastrous than clever.

In the final analysis, neutralism means freedom for any imperialism to implant itself in Africa. In view of the discreteness of African economies, it means freedom to stake out the continent with outposts and various zones of influence. We realize that neutralism, which is doubtless tenable on the scale of a great African nation not yet formed, is reduced to dangerous opportunism when practiced by small nations or dwarf states subject to the temptation of outbidding each other instead of presenting a united front to resist the new

84

strategies of domination. Narrow nationalisms reflect a lack of historical perspective and are surely ill-advised when they hope to guarantee the development of the economies they want to liberate by suddenly reversing their policies, by skillful maneuvering, or by changing partners. The road to real African independence, constructed on the solid rock of a strong economy, lies not so much in neutralism as in large regroupings that permit the concentration of poles, centers, and axes of development. That is why Mali will be an open nation that must expand to fulfill its role.

Secondly, let us remember that to become a reality, decolonization must be accompanied by a transformation of structures, economic ones particularly. It is not enough to have a national state, a national government, a national superstructure; it is necessary to promote a progressive national policy for the entire collectivity. In the examples discussed, we have proved that growth is not development, in neither the human nor the collective sense of the word. There is really no development—that is to say, collective creation, in the service of the community—unless the production techniques employed, no matter how perfect, have succeeded in integrating the most important sectors of the nation within the economic system. There is really no development if the raising of production and consumption levels—if the progress accomplished—is restricted to a few privileged individuals, even if these be citizens. Properly speaking, there is no development of an independent economy—in so far as that can exist—without a network of economic, financial, and technical facilities, and above all, without a total reconversion of relationships between evolved economies and younger economies—of whichever camp, of whichever ideology. We now know that neither the examples taken from the socialist camp nor those from the capitalist camp can serve as models without serious modification or thorough and profound readaptation. We know that even industrialization, so necessary for the modernization of the economy, is not a sufficient guarantee against the effects of domination when it proceeds by complementary investments or when it only creates factories for raw materials, poorly linked to the country. We know that despite the socialist brotherhood repeatedly proclaimed, the rules governing trade still rest on the principle of the greatest profit for the dominant economy.

But we are no less convinced—far from it—of the weaknesses of the capitalist camp, the impotence of its methods, the senility of its institutions. Its solutions cannot satisfy us. We realize the necessity for proceeding on the ruins of colonialism to a "creative destruction" that must precede the birth of a national mass economy. Otherwise, we condemn ourselves to perpetuate domestic imbalance and to maintain underdevelopment, despite political changes and the appearance of economic prosperity, if only the prosperity of the capitalist sector. Decolonization in its economic aspect is the replacement of old relationships—based on force and on ruses that are again trying to gain headway—with a fruitful dialogue between economies that share a common solidarity. This is why the doctrine of an emergent nation such as ours cannot be one of an exclusive, unilateral development, but rather—to quote François Perroux—one of "mutual development." In other words, economic problems can no longer be envisaged through the lenses of the politicians, but from the viewpoint of world solidarity.

III

The Mali Experiment
or
A New Technique of Development

9

THE DISCOVERY OF THE *TIERS-MONDE* AND SCIENCES OF DEVELOPMENT

WITH THE DISCOVERY of the *Tiers-Monde,* the science of development has made considerable progress these last few years. One of the most enriching aspects of the revolution in this domain is the discovery of the specific economic vocation of each of the various civilizations. Hitherto, many had insisted—and still insist, with some justification—on the influence of foreign civilizations as dominant cultures on the economic structures of the dominated societies, and the resulting repercussions on social structures. Henceforth, attention will be focused on the role of the economy as a criterion of civilization, thus offering the economist a new perspective that snatches him from cold scientific orthodoxy to make of him what he really is: a humanist. The reference to the universality of the basic laws of economics remains valid in large measure, but more and more it seems that economic analysis gains from being practiced by diverse civilizations that do not of necessity share the same economic ideals or attitudes, and that do not have the same type of organization. On the contrary, all that we know of *Tiers-Monde* civilizations indicates their rejection of the economic symbolism of the West.

A few examples will illustrate this elementary truth. Among Indian and African civilizations, which are essentially spiritualistic, the idea of economic utility is appreciated otherwise than in the old or young materialistic civilizations, or civilizations issuing from formative processes where, in spite of spiritual factors, the materialistic element dominates. This is true of Western civilizations, which resemble one another in this respect, whatever ideological divergences—as profound as Christianity and atheism—may oppose them. There, no doubt, is where we must seek an explanation for the apparently paradoxical fact that Soviet Russia feels herself to be the daughter of the same mother as Catholic France: the concept of utility is interpreted in the same way by Western countries so different in political, economic, and social regimes. Despite the differences that split them today into two distinct, antagonistic worlds, economic utility arouses in both of them the same psychological complex and is inscribed in a uniform context of values. It is understandable that the reactions it provokes on both sides are similar and that its analysis can be deduced from the same principles. By the same token, it is understandable that the reception of this "concept" is more or less identical in Asian or African societies, despite the progress of Westernism caused by the interpenetration of civilizations.

Utility for an African or Asian is determined less by rational, concrete elements than by a kind of intuitive fear, with individual interests dissolving in the totality of group interests. It is necessary to start from this ontological conception of utility to understand why it is so difficult for African or Asian civilizations—especially the former—disturbed by Occidental influences, to accept the monetary symbolism of the West and the fetishism of money that is the great tyranny of civilizations considered advanced. Born to affirm a system of values unrelated to the value of money, the non-Western civilizations of Africa and Asia could only produce relationships in which monetary considerations always remain secondary.

Since economy is essentially based on human and social relations, since it is in essence socialistic, in the broadest sense of the term, the rule of the accumulation of money—the foundation of capitalism—cannot be the law that will determine the formation of structures in such civilizations. The economist who wishes to do a scientific job, to make an analysis that goes to the heart of reality, can no longer be content with established schemata, fixed norms, prefabricated models. Trying to discover the intimate nature of things, to grasp facts in all their complexity, he will formulate valid rules, deduce specific laws that will explain the elaboration of the economies studied and enable them to establish the conditions of their growth. We know today, thanks to the laborious investigations of the historical school, that economic development must be considered as a long, patient advance down through the ages, a tortuous historical process involving different forms of economies that are only ephemeral.

One of the principal contemporary representatives of this thinking, the historian W. W. Rostow, has recently extended the analysis by distinguishing five stages in the growth of nations, five steps that are only a series of "development stages," registered in a general evolution. In the first stage we meet traditional society with its equally traditional economy, whose dominant sector is agriculture. Far from static, it possesses an internal dynamism, limited by the rudimentary character of the techniques, by social structures that leave little room for "vertical mobility." On a higher level are societies and economies of the transitory stage, marked by fundamental transformations of structures caused by modifications of the political system and production techniques. The decisive criterion is the increase in rate of investment, which conditions the increase in per capita production. All this sets in play a certain number of factors, some psychological or human, such as the aptitude to support the efforts and risks that every innovation entails, and the aptitude to utilize useful inventions. Other factors are purely economic, such as development of the primary sector and of basic services. Still other factors are social and political, such as social coalitions formed by nationalism.

> In Germany it was certainly a nationalism based on past humiliation and future hope that did the job . . . the Junkers and the men of the East, more than the men of trade and the liberals of the West. In Russia it was a series of military intrusions and defeats, stretching out over a century, that was the great engine of change: Napoleon's invasion, the Crimean War, the Russo-Japanese War, and then, finally, the First World War. In Japan it was the effect not of high profits or manufactured consumers' goods but of the Opium War in China in the early 1840's and Commodore Peary's seven black ships a decade later that cast the die for modernization.[1]

This preparatory period is followed by a crucial stage, the "take-off," marked by a radical change in the rate of investment, a radical modification of structures that makes growth almost automatic. Yet, to assure the take-off, one needs sufficient financial resources, the source of which can be found

[1] W. W. Rostow, *The Stages of Economic Growth* (London and New York: Cambridge University Press, 1960), p. 27.

either in such techniques for raising government revenues as have been employed by India and Communist China; or by inflation, as in Great Britain in 1790, the United States in 1850, and Japan in 1870; or by the increase in exports, as indicated by the examples of American, Russian, and Canadian wheat, Japanese silk, and Swedish paper pulp during the take-off of the economy of these countries. It will be necessary to add to the system of raising capital the creation of key sectors of basic industries, since the evolving societies do not need to reproduce the structural succession of Great Britain, the United States, or Russia.

The last stage of this evolution is the maturity resulting from the accumulation of acquired technical skills and producing substantial real income, between $400 and $600, with a rapidly increasing urban population, stronger and stronger social pressures, a highly bureaucratized power of direction, more and more unbearable human costs; in brief, a "dangerous period, at the same time rich in new and promising choices." This schema cannot fail to impress any mind placed in a historical perspective to study the phenomena of economic development. Its essential merit is that it does not isolate these phenomena but integrates them in the general evolution of humanity. One will also be grateful to it for pointing out, en route, the importance of social, human, and political factors in the elaboration of the different types of economy and the disarticulations that their transformations require. Thus it enriches economic analysis, especially that of the *Tiers-Monde*, whose processes the old methods of analysis cannot explain.

It is no exaggeration to claim that the science of development owes its present depth to this theory, while the dynamic leaders of economy owe their new techniques to it. From it the emergent nations can learn useful lessons. They will discover the variety of choices offered them to effect their take-off and progress toward maturity. This choice can lead to concentrated efforts in a given economic sector; or, on occasion, it may simply consist in the use of psychological or moral forces, as Switzerland, Israel, and Hong Kong have exemplified by attaining a high level of industrialization without important natural resources. The wide range of solutions must convince the leaders of the young states that they should stop trying to imitate at any price the most spectacular experiences—American, German, or Russian—while other experiences—that of Sweden, for example—would prove more instructive. But all these interesting data will not lead us to enclose our economic construction in the rigid framework of a predetermined evolution. It matters little, in any case, to know whether a given economy—Mali's, for example—has passed successfully through the stages mentioned, or even if it has reached the stage of maturity. The essential thing is to be sure that the take-off is initiated, not only for growth, but for a balanced expansion—an authentic development.

GROWTH AND DEVELOPMENT

At this point in our analysis, it is useful to recall the distinction between growth and development. This is less a question of vocabulary than a fundamental problem. As we have just seen, colonial capitalism built growing economies. On becoming independent, Morocco and Tunisia inherited economies in full expansion. This is because growth is especially a phenomenon of structural transformations and there

94

is no doubt that capitalism effected the structural transformations of traditional economies. Such growth is also the "passage from one system to another system," from one "type of organization to another." There is growth when an economy passes from a self-sufficient to a market economy, from the communal to the capitalist type of organization, with worldwide augmentation over a long period. This is the phenomenon that we have observed everywhere on examining the evolution of the economies of politically dependent countries. This could also be detected on studying the economies of the West African states under the impulse of European capitalism.

Furthermore, this growth is accompanied by numerous indications of progress. It is analyzed, finally, as a phenomenon applicable "to any factor or to any ascending result of various factors. One speaks of population growth, growth in equipment, growth in savings, growth in investments, growth in employment, growth in national income. Without qualification, growth is economic growth considered as a whole. It is interpreted by an ascending number (gross product, net earnings). One pays no attention to the structure of production; in fact, growth may conceal an increasing imbalance and underlie a recession."[2] Thus defined, growth is not development, that is, the process of creating a progressive economy, and engendering social and human progress. It does not suffice to replace archaic structures by those of a capitalistic mercantile economy. It is not enough to create a process of capital accumulation and important investments. Nor is it sufficient to replace an improvised type of organization with

[2] L. J. Lebret, *Sciences economiques et développement* (Paris: Economie et humanisme, 1958), II, 23.

a complex type, or rudimentary techniques with advanced ones. It is necessary that the structural modifications, the contribution of capital, the introduction of new types of organization and superior techniques be translated into a true integration of the national economy with the various strata of the population. It is on this condition, which presupposes the progressive disappearance of internal imbalance, that we may speak of balanced expansion, of development. While the concept of growth implies a somewhat static aspect and sets in motion a mercantile process, the concept of development evokes, on the contrary, a process of dynamic creation, an *élan* toward progressive integration employing a system of effective liaisons and transmissions of progress.

In sum, ". . . development is situated along the lines of a co-ordinated growth, of a rational integration of resources, of a higher standard of living and culture for the population, particularly for the rural and urban masses. Development is continuous growth attuned to human valorization."[3] It is something different from expansion, which is growth in power and can result from an outside will "threatening either domestic economic balance or autonomy, or both at the same time." In Mali and elsewhere, we have expansion especially of industrial sectors without a corresponding expansion of the small and medium enterprises or—a still more significant fact—an expansion of the stagnant agricultural sector. According to the formula of the *Economie et Humanisme* group,[4] development is "the passage of the totality of subpopulations

---

[3] Lebret, *op. cit.*, p. 24.

[4] The *Economie et Humanisme* (Economy and Humanism) group, directed by Father Lebret, recently made the inventory of Senegal's resources that served as a basis for that country's development plan.—Tr.

inhabiting a country from a less human to a more human living standard, at the least expense to labor and capital, and at the fastest possible rhythm." For an underdeveloped country, it is the passage from a technically and culturally inferior to a technically and culturally superior phase. In this respect, Sweden represents the most striking example.

To start the process of development in economies of retarded growth like ours, the first objective must be to suppress structural obstacles that hamper development. Thus one will understand the importance that we attach to the reform of Mali's economic structures inherited from colonial capitalism. It will be vain to hope for a profound change toward a progressive economy—guaranteeing the minimal conditions of life to the nation, creating conditions for a market on a scale to meet our needs—without a bold restructuration incompatible with an exaggerated desire to spare the former capitalist structures. But the inner dynamism, the creative capacity, will not suffice to spark the process of development. We will need investments, poles of development, networks of trade—all of which are items that force us out of our isolation—to proceed to relations with more developed economies. However, we must be careful lest these relations reinforce dependence. On the contrary, they must be affirmed as an element of progress, thanks to the effects of the growth impulse, which will help in the change of structures and types of organization, and will inspire induced investment, induced consumption, and induced innovations. This will all be realized in a milieu favorable to diffusion because it will have been previously prepared. This means that after independence, if we intend to start a process of development on behalf of Mali's economy, we cannot hesitate to establish connections with the older French economy, whose poles of development can play a crucial role for us.

At the same time, we shall strengthen our ties with the economies of neighboring sister countries, which—by the market, the network of trade, and the zones and points of development that they offer—are factors of progress not to be neglected. And yet, so that the new experience will not reproduce the colonial capitalist experience, it is important to break the old ties, to review economic relations, to substitute a new spirit for the former mentality, and, more concretely, to reconvert the functions performed at poles of development. The latter must stop being "great dominant units," installed to procure advantages for the developed economy to the detriment of the emergent economy, or great international firms localized on the national territory but functionally foreign to our economy. In other words, whether implanted or not in Mali's geographical area, the poles of development must be focal areas of economic, social, and cultural progress, and not simply points of polarization, exerting their influence over too limited an area and worsening the distortions instead of correcting them. We shall be realistic enough not to require the abolition of the idea of profit or to dream of an economy founded on the unselfishness of nations. But we shall take care to replace the selfishness of rich nations that have a one-sided conception of development with a truly co-operative spirit that will make development a two-way street on which —in accordance with a law of reciprocity—the related economies, the less developed as well as the more developed, can evolve a perpetual dialogue.

Mutual Development, or the Dialogue Between Nations of Good Will

The concept of mutual development that we owe to François Perroux—along with so many other precious tools of analysis—provides the solution that will reconcile the conflicting interests of East and West, capitalist and communist, and ward off the structural dangers of imperialism they threaten. This concept will also lessen the threat of violent opposition between rich nations and poor nations. It is necessary to describe its mechanism, its method of application, and its spirit to appreciate its full scope in a world confused by the ineffectiveness of systems that strive so bitterly for hegemony. A group of nations—unequally developed technically and culturally, aware of the unreality of development in the narrow framework of projects territorially limited, with means strictly circumscribed by domestic possibilities—decides rationally and deliberately, by common accord, to undertake a collective experiment of open co-operation. It will be noted at once that the basis of the enterprise is both the mutual consent of the partners freely given, and the determination to pursue the common experiment over a period necessary for its fruition.

The older, or pilot, nation—France in this instance—places at the disposal of the sister nations seeking development its knowledge, its production and organizational techniques (capital being only one and not the essential one of these), its poles, centers, and axes of development. This participation in the attempted collective experiment involves certain basic requirements for the elder nation. It will not be enough to define its position negatively by proclaiming the abolition of former relationships and a break with all imperialisms. It must positively resolve to contribute to the elaboration of new relationships. The solution for the elder nation cannot consist of a withdrawal intended to be realistic but actually fatal, leading rapidly to obliteration. The solution is for it to be more effective than ever, in order to be more present than ever in the world and especially in the zone of solidarity involved. To face up to its responsibilities, it must work to assist in the rapid preparation of technical and administrative elites summoned to apply the doctrine of a "nation with limited sovereignty." It must increase its economic capacities, improve its processes, and reform its own structures to adapt them to the new requirements.

On this basis the solidarity of the pilot nation and its affiliates will have real meaning, and become a solid rampart against any schisms threatened by the inevitable rivalry of outside competition. If France is to play her role as economic leader in this peaceful coalition intended to be an example of effective co-operation, she cannot remain what she is: a great nation anachronistically attached to liberalism and yet subjected, even in her relations with allied nations, to pressures from economic and financial groups. For France to become a pilot nation in the perspective of an evolving Community and in the present world context, a profound reconversion is necessary. This raises questions about the necessity of producing for the associated sister nations a spokesman other than capitalism. As François Perroux notes:

This state of affairs that has characterized colonial capitalism does not disappear—on the contrary—when legal and nominal sovereignty is acquired by a country, without changing the concentration of economic and financial means. The difficulty worsens when the state principally interested in the overseas territory is itself not free from pressure by its own capitalists.

This is all the less susceptible to piecemeal correction because transfers of capital and trade from the danger points to those less dangerous remain at the disposal of the financial groups and of their states. Capitalism's maneuverability on the world scale is reduced but not destroyed by the progress of communism.

Under these conditions, tragic to any observer who is neither too distracted nor absolutely dishonest, there is posed the question of relations between the industrial and the political powers in the Western camp, more precisely, in our Community. The homelands and nations are threatened by monopolistic capitalism, which certain people call the most favorable regime for freedom.[5]

In other words, a policy of mutual development requires France to make institutional changes leading to an original socialism, to set up effective controls on the great businesses, and to liquidate camouflaged "colonialist" capitalism. Obviously, for the pilot nation the effectiveness of mutual development consists not only in material advantages of the classic type in the development of its own trade, but especially in the general possibilities of renewal that it offers, and in the vitalizing forces that it contributes to this permanent dialogue between free nations. For the young nations that have just recovered their independence, the acceptance of the experiment with the ex-colonizing nations indicates that they have overcome the colonized complex that makes one live in perpetual insecurity. The agreement also signifies that they

[5] *Les Nations en voie de se faire,* lecture delivered at the Collège de France, pp. 207–8.

accept the limits imposed on all partners in every collective enterprise. To consent to these inevitable restrictions is not to lose one's sovereignty, but rather to establish it under conditions that will allow it to be fully enjoyed. These restrictions actually strengthen sovereignty, by removing it from isolation and enabling it to benefit from all the authority of a unified group.

The twentieth-century societies afflicted by nationalist vertigo need to be constantly reminded that:

> . . . the national state no longer procures security and prosperity easily for its nationals. Since national sovereignties are severely limited, both the inhabitants and the countries involved seek greater protection and well-being in zones of political co-operation that group several nations within multinational industrial regions. As far as means are concerned, no partial economy could be satisfied with its potential, whereas a global economy offers a chance of better results, by organizing all men and resources judiciously in the aim of satisfying all human aspirations and needs.
>
> Self-determination of partial groupings is limited by self-determination of all humanity. The sovereign nation and the national state will rightly yield to other political formations whenever the latter bring us closer to the ideal model, where each nation agrees to limit itself for the purpose of serving its sister nation and all mankind.[6]

Young nations, like colonial imperialists of yore, will be tempted to have a unilateral and, therefore, a narrow conception of development that will want to consider only services received or expected, thus transforming solidarity into a new market of dupes, whose bargaining position will be

[6] *Ibid.*, p. 192.

hardly more tolerable than before. On the contrary, to base relations on mutual respect of the partners, it will be advisable to establish reciprocity rather than inequality, in exchanges of services. The new dialogue that must be substituted for the old relationships, if it is to be really fruitful, will surely banish any spirit of submission as well as the mentality of begging and of profiteering. In this perspective, mutual development will require the pilot nation and its associates to pool great natural resources, their exploitation, and the utilization of poles of development. This implies on both sides—especially on the side of young nationalisms, where the temptation is so great—the abandonment of attitudes of territorial chauvinism, of easy recourse to procedures of nationalization, and of improvisation of currency systems or zones of prestige, without any economic significance. This presupposes on the part of the young states a real political maturity, which is essential to economic maturity. In this dialogue between nations resolved to pursue in common such an original experiment, where there is no room for subterfuge or ambiguity, the golden rule must be the realism of the partners. Mutual development will not suppress structural imbalance all at once, as if by a magic wand, and establish without effort a harmony between the affiliated national economies. It should permit, however, their development in a framework that is economically and technically valid. It should guarantee the progressive reduction of imbalances in order to make them bearable. This result remains inaccessible to zones of solidarity where other formulas are applied, even when they claim to be inspired by scientific socialism. To forestall recriminations or regrets, it must be understood that mutual development does not mean the end of difficulties between nations that choose this road by common consent.

As a technique of growth, it implies a de-mystified collaboration "containing a minimum of inequalities or, more exactly, admitting inequalities required and justified from the point of view of the common interest of the elder country and the retarded countries." It is also a policy—that is, a compromise—resulting not from an imposed treaty, but from a contract freely negotiated for the purpose of promoting the development of a backward economy by means of a conscious, reasoned solidarity. As a dialogue, it substitutes interlocutors for "passive receivers," partners for docile instruments, freed men for wards. And from this open, permanent dialogue—surely destined to become animated because it is alive—one hopes that there will come agreement on the essential points: formation of cadres, allocation of work and enterprise, the choice of investments able to induce gross effects, the duty of the retarded country to discuss the "capitalist tempo and to substitute its own," the problem of the localization of investments, and finally, the attainment of the accepted model, by means of a development plan. The latter, the keystone of mutual development, opens new prospects for retarded nations by fixing objectives less concerned with rates of global growth than with "a structural preference"; by combating the concentration of investments, and fighting for "integration" and "partial disintegrations" within zones; and by establishing dialogues between groups and regions that, abandoned to themselves, would be victims of their local particularisms.

Thus, because of mutual development that obviously will be more fruitful than the promises of parallel development, the economic future appears, not in isolation, but in a common perspective. The language of domination gives way to a confident dialogue, gift economy is transferred into a collective economy "where each one finds the wherewithal to recognize himself as an equal."[7]

[7] Emile Roche, "Risques et chances d'une Communauté," *Revue des deux Mondes,* March 1, 1960.

10

MALI: A REGIONAL LINK IN THE WORLD ECONOMY

THE EXPERIMENT of independent Mali, within a multinational community adopting France as pilot nation, is an application of the technique of mutual development. It is an act of faith in the efficacy of the dialogue as an interrelational policy, in preference to violence and sterile disputes. It is a reasonably optimistic wager on the future relationships between dominant and dominated economies, between ex-colonizers and ex-colonized, and in general, between developed countries and countries with retarded growth. As a model of national construction anticipating a collective economy—according to a process of expansion by concentric circles of solidarity—Mali is not only a hope, a doctrine, but a method of universalizing the economy, a "regional link" on the dangerous road to the global economy of the twentieth century.

Independence and solidarity—these are the two great principles on which the Mali government rests. It is an independence not only desirable but necessary, to assure the indispensable self-determination that alone can justify the dialogue, normalize relations, and authenticate co-operation. But it must be a de-mystified independence that, conscious of twentieth-century realities, accepts limited sovereignty in order to integrate the nation within a larger movement. The solidarity is essential so that independence may become a tangible reality by its economic content—an assured and not a protected independence. But this solidarity with which Mali affirms its independence means to be both vertical and horizontal. In other words, Mali's economy aspires to be at once a continental and a transcontinental economy, thanks to its judiciously established temporal and spatial links, thanks to its rational start on the mechanism of concentric circles of solidarity that obey the law of mutual development. Because it is motivated by such prospects, the Mali experiment becomes an example of world-wide import; its effects on history are difficult to predict. We shall describe its essential aspects by analyzing the Franco-Malian agreements concerning economic and financial relations, and by indicating Mali's plans for building a continental and subsequently a world economy. Preceding the study of these prospects, we shall examine Mali's economic situation on the eve of independence.

THE ECONOMY OF MALI ON THE EVE OF INDEPENDENCE

First, what is Mali? Constitutionally speaking, it is not a unitary state, but a federation of states comprising two republics, Senegal and the Sudan, which, after the referendum of October, 1958, adopted a common political choice: independence and unity. Despite the oppositions created by colonization and accentuated by the evolution introduced by the *loi-cadre*,[1] which stressed the affirmation of the territorial personality, the tendency to regroup won out in both countries,

---

[1] This much-discussed law of 1956 provided certain advantages, such as universal suffrage, to French African territories, but at the same time contributed to their Balkanization by dividing French West Africa and French Equatorial Africa into semiautonomous units.—Tr.

because the inflexible will of their leaders was sustained by the whole working population. The Sudan and Senegal shared the same historical origins, belonged to the same area of traditional civilization. These elements of *rapprochement,* without eliminating the diversity of temperaments, of territorial psychologies, and organizational techniques, finally established the idea of a common national conscience. A political reality, founded on historical and cultural bases and on common options, Mali is also a coherent, viable economic reality—much more, in any event, than certain unions that have no common denominator except an infantile dream of annexation.

Mali's great luck is in the complementary nature of the two economies, Senegalese and Sudanese; although both are agricultural, they are structurally different. The policy of capital concentration around ports—a favorite policy of colonial capitalism—explains, as everywhere else, the disparity in the implantation of industries within the federal territory. But Senegal is perfectly aware of the fact that if its port and industries are to survive, it needs the minimum economic area of the Sudan, while anticipating a rapid broadening of this area. The Niger Office, in order to continue to produce rice and cotton, knows that it must depend on the market of its sister republic. If there is structural disequilibrium between the two affiliated economies, we may say that this is a tolerable and even a useful imbalance, imposing on the two states the necessity for mutual development. Thus the duality of structures, instead of causing competition and difficulties, motivates co-operation. An economic reality founded on the complementary nature of its components, Mali is also a market—not a large market with its 6 million consumers, but none-

108

theless a market able to sustain honorably comparison with other markets formed along territorial lines. Its great weakness consists less in the relative smallness of its market (which can be remedied), less in the inadequate development of the industrial sector or the uneven character of this development throughout the national territory, than in the absence of any real pole of development.

The recent petroleum discoveries, the mining prospects in the Kéniéba region of the Sudan, do not yet justify the hope of implanting great propulsive forces in Mali. The deficiency of energy resources, along with the absence of minerals, postpones for an undetermined future the era of great industrial complexes in Mali. These serious deficiencies must be borne in mind to appreciate fully the limits of an economic development that might try to confine itself within the framework of Mali's possibilities. They force us to seek actively the collaboration of neighboring states, and especially of France, a friendly republic whose poles of development must stop functioning principally for the profit of French economy and work for the ensemble, according to the process of mutual development.

Having said that, we shall be careful not to blacken the picture unduly, in so far as developmental prospects are concerned. Though it is true that Mali has no propulsive force at the moment, at least it possesses important advantages: among others, two great river basins that are large arteries for trade in a revitalized economy, three openings on the sea that, along with Dakar, are irreplaceable trade centers by reason of their geographical position. Endowed with modern production centers, Mali takes justifiable pride in having a potential focal point of progress as its capital. After having brought down upon itself so many criticisms and recriminations, Dakar is destined to be—by its economic, social, and cultural infra-structure, and by the commercial currents that still converge there—the hub from which the benefits of mutual development will radiate toward the groups that today are most hostile to it. If it were only by this contribution, Mali's vocation would seem amply justified.

A microanalytical examination of Mali's structures, although certain to be incomplete at the present stage of our research, seems to us indispensable to determine valid solutions, after a precise diagnosis has been made. Though Mali is the most industrialized country of all West Africa; though it has power units of small and moderate dimensions that can be the point of departure for a process of chain reactions favorable to development; though Mali enjoys the implantation on its national territory of focal points of progress, whose radiance, already evident, may become dazzlingly brilliant to-morrow, the fact remains that our economy is still of the colonial type and retarded, despite three years of semi-au-tonomy and internal autonomy.

This admission, inspired by a constant desire for scientific objectivity, is not to be construed as a kind of self-condemna-tion. This would be jumping to conclusions and forgetting the examples studied earlier of independent African or Asian countries that have not yet resolved—not by any means—the problems of economic dependence by thoroughgoing struc-tural transformation. Nor are we recalling this to ease our conscience or even to justify ourselves, but simply to say that we have a right to expect an indulgence at least equal to that accorded others by our censors. Nevertheless, despite the long-established European capitalism, despite the existence of an industrial sector with a modernism reflecting the boldness of private initiative (more responsible than the colonial state for economic creation), we must note the maintenance by and large of the structures of market economy, that is, the mercantile economy of capitalist profit for which the local economy is not a primary consideration. It is significant that despite all the talk of socialism, and though the death knell of imperialism has sounded in the congresses of all political parties, labor unions, and youth organizations, the problem remains as alive as ever. In Senegal, for example, in this year of grace 1960—notwithstanding the efforts of the government—traditional trade controls a sector as vital as that of peanuts. There are still organisms managed by oligopolistic groups that control unsupervised the import trade in essential consumers' goods. By means of this double dependence, foreign mercantile capitalism remains the real master of the game and wins at every turn, even more so than industrial capitalism. Understandably, the government has resolved, despite the difficulties that lie ahead, to remedy this situation, which has lasted long enough and which cannot be prolonged without discrediting the party responsible, forever and entirely.

The market economy, common to Senegal and the Sudan, is also, like all economies of this type, a nonintegrated economy, with competing sectors, annulling the effects of over-all economic progress that could result from such public and private investment as the approximate 78 billion francs in the period 1948–57.[2] Therefore, an economy of inhuman growth utilizes an important sum of capital while unfortunately neg-

[2] G. Le Hegarat, "Essai d'un tableau économique de la Fédération du Mali," *Bulletin de la Banque Centrale des Etats de l'Afrique de l'ouest* (Dakar: February, 1960).

lecting the masses. No doubt the policies pursued during re-cent years on behalf of the peasantry lessen the effects of these structures on standards of living, on housing, on demographic evolution, and on per capita income. The surveys now being conducted promise favorable results in this area. But the dominant feature remains the persistence of structures of an economy that has not yet attained the phase of creative de-struction that must precede the take-off of a progressive na-tional economy. It is true that this structural transformation is hampered by the existence of middle classes and a local *bour-geoisie,* products and subproducts of the established system, which finds in these elements influential allies and important pressure groups. The resistance thus formed cannot be mini-mized, as the nation's leaders are obliged to restrain a politi-cal opposition that, while claiming to be leftist, stands ready to ally itself with all backward forces. All these difficulties make no less urgent the need for the party in power to fight courageously against the system of market economy, with a view to advancing the economy of independent Mali. ✓ stop

This explains the administrative reforms undertaken by the Senegalese government that have utilized competent young cadres in the construction of a decentralized and democratized superstructure, dividing the country into seven large regions corresponding to economic entities. These regions are them-selves divided into districts and departments. The innovations include: economic reforms placing in the hands of the gov-ernment the financial and economic levers of the country, creating a Development Bank and an Office to Commercialize Agricultural Output; regional centers to aid development and replace organizations falsely co-operative and falsely demo-cratic; centers for rural expansion aiming to promote, in col-

112

laboration with the regional development centers, an authentic co-operative sector to start the rural areas on the road to economic and social progress; the creation of a housing fund that will serve both rural and urban sectors; the reactivation of old agricultural projects in regions hitherto neglected by the supporters of the capitalist economy. Having fulfilled this precondition, one can envisage the future of our economic development optimistically, thanks to the utilization, during the euphoria of independence, of a long-term master plan, established not according to prefabricated models or foreign imitations but on the basis of our actual needs, our real potential, and our own conception of development.

Understanding this, Mali's leaders decided to take advantage of the legal possibilities of internal autonomy and to draw up long-term regional development plans without waiting for complete independence. The preparation of these plans is entrusted to developmental experts who use different methods of analysis. (It may prove difficult to adjust them.) The plans tend to establish a probable development for each state, after determining its needs scientifically and taking inventory of its total resources. This is the first time in Black Africa that such a basic job has been done. And the result will not be the least important contribution of the present leaders.

It is regrettable that the evolution of political structures has not permitted from the very beginning the establishment of a plan for the whole Federation. And especially, as noted earlier, is it to be regretted that the analyses of the two federated states have not been assigned to the same team of experts. This would unquestionably have facilitated the indispensable co-ordination and the preparation of a federal

113

plan. But perhaps this diversity of methods will be a source of enrichment rather than of irreconcilable divergences, as might be feared. What is unique in the history of newly independent countries is that for the first time, a nation reaches this ultimate stage not empty-handed, but provided with a tool for development, perfectly aware of its needs, deficiencies, and potential, and knowing exactly which road it must follow to realize its destiny. What is positive is that Mali presents itself, at the rendezvous of giving and receiving, cognizant of what it can give and what it wants to receive, bringing to the debate between nations a definite program that eliminates ambiguities and sterile hesitations.

Now we must provide some information concerning Mali's economic situation, in order to form an exact idea of the tasks awaiting us after independence. We shall be forced to settle for approximate estimates, since the rupture of the former group of territories produced, among other evils, the dislocation of statistical services and impeded the establishment of new ones, adequately equipped, for Mali if not for the individual states of former French West Africa. Let us add at once that we do not intend to draw up a balance sheet or to describe an evolution over so short a period, inasmuch as Mali is scarcely one year old. It is rather a matter of detecting a trend, of charting a course—no matter how vague—of an evolution that requires our full attention from the outset.

The main characteristic is the dependence of Mali's economy on a single export commodity: peanuts. These represent nine-tenths of the sales to a single customer, France, which buys them at a price higher than the world market rate. We are equally dependent on imports. Here our de-

114

pendence is less obvious but no less real. Three-fourths of Mali's purchases come from the franc zone. We are likewise dependent in trade, as indicated by a structural deficit in our trade balance of one-third of the imports, or 12–15 billion francs. And, finally, we are dependent on investments and capital movements. The metropolitan treasury pays Mali large sums in the form of salaries. It is estimated that in Senegal, military expenditures amount to almost 10 billion francs. This helps to stabilize the national income and emphasizes the consequences of a mass evacuation of French troops, an evacuation justifiably rejected by Mali's leaders. On the other hand, private capital, taking advantage of the liberal regime and, moreover, encouraged by the overvalued exchange rate, had a field day transferring funds, thus maintaining debilitating "hemorrhages" of foreign exchange. According to a recent study made by M. de Bernis for Mali's negotiators, one can establish, for the year 1957, the balance of payments as follows:

	(billion francs)
Public transfers	+22
Private transfers	—26
Settlement of trade deficit	—16
Transfer of capital without commercial cause	—10
Levy on franc reserves of the Central Bank of West African States	— 4

According to the same author, transfers of private capital without commercial cause increased by 48 per cent between 1957 and 1958, from —9,563 million francs to —14,151 million. Thus the participation of the metropolitan government in the effort toward investment was singularly offset "by the rules of the monetary and commercial play" that tend

115

to strengthen dependence. Here we find once again the consequences of the mechanics of colonial capitalism, more anxious to accumulate profits than to innovate creatively, a prisoner of defensive reflexes that leave no room for rational currency conversion. It will be observed, somewhat regretfully, that neither the reassurances of the Mali authorities nor concrete measures to stimulate private investment have been able to overcome the psychosis of the private sector, for which independence always looms as a direct threat. This fear is evidently not entirely unjustified when, confronting a fiercely conservative capitalism, the leaders hope to inculcate a will for regeneration and a desire to build an economy in the service of the nation.

Despite this obvious dependence, Mali's economy is relatively well prepared for the test of independence. It has the advantage of a number of administrative, psychological, and political preconditions, thanks to the foresight of the nation's leaders, who made good use of the periods of semiautonomy and autonomy. Thus Mali has a superstructure that doubtless needs to be gradually perfected, but that already shows promise of being effective. Already there are groups of technicians, and more will be recruited in increasing numbers. Mali's economy arouses the enthusiasm of the public, the sympathy of the foreigner. It inspires vocations and excites healthy passions; it is already a dynamic factor for the entire nation. After tumultuous clashes, it has won the support of governments and trade-unions; it has become a center of national interest.

In a word, it is being born under the conditions that forge great destinies. There is no doubt that Mali's economy, notwithstanding unquestionable weaknesses, will support the vocation of a nation strong because it is united.

THE NEW FRANCO-MALIAN RELATIONS: A BRIEF ANALYSIS OF THE ECONOMIC AND FINANCIAL AGREEMENTS

On attaining its independence, Mali insisted on making it an effective tool for development. Thus it was eager to give its new relations with France an original orientation to reconcile independence and interdependence. This imperative applies to its relations not only with the former Metropole, but especially with the emergent West African nations. As a sovereign nation, Mali, in its new relationships with France, will control its foreign trade, in so far as this sovereignty is possible for any nation, large or small, in this interdependent world. It has the right to print its own money, like any sovereign nation, and the power to join any zone of solidarity it pleases or to create its own monetary zone if such should be its desire or in its interests.

For its trade it chooses the partners it wishes. It is master of its fiscal setup; it controls credit and capital movements. It fixes the status of investments, draws up its plan, and decides on the details of its execution; it discusses the means of financing the plan, in line with national objectives. But being a "solidarity nation," Mali seeks its development within a zone of solidarity, the technical framework of which is called the "franc zone" and the institutional framework, the "Community." Having accepted the dialogue not only with France, but with the sister states of the Community—by reason of its option for African unity—it cannot use its rights to define its political and financial policy, or to initiate such policies, without considering the possible repercussions on its partners'

117

economies. Thus it must agree to consultations, to discussions, which alone will assure the synchronization of the various attitudes. This dialogue, elevated to the position of an institution, will take place at the summit, at periodic conferences between chiefs of state and governments, and on a lower level, within specialized technical organizations. Having chosen freely to assume its development in a definite zone of solidarity—the franc zone—Mali willingly renounces having its own currency and central bank for the time being. It refuses to yield to the easy temptation of deceptive display for the pleasure of affirming a spurious sovereignty. It knows that the possession of a monetary system is no guarantee of independence, that there are dominant and dominated currencies, and that the struggle between the two blocs rests basically on the hegemony of two currencies: the dollar and the ruble. All other national currencies, including the recalcitrant pound sterling, are only economic satellites. Mali realizes that in addition to the technical problems arising from placing a national currency in circulation, there is for a young state venturing along this road the fearful temptation to overexpand the money supply and thus to expose the economy to monetary measures that may have disastrous consequences at home and abroad.

The fact of the matter is that for Mali, it is a question of fostering a conception of a monetary zone more in keeping with evolution—that of the franc zone, no longer specifically a monetarist zone,[3] but more precisely a zone of growth and development. Not the least significant contribution of the

[3] According to Professor Perroux, a "monetarist zone is not an area purely and simply defined by a common currency, but based on a common growth and development policy."—Tr.

118

Mali delegation was its successful sponsorship of this viewpoint, which preserves the unity of the Community. Obviously, the failure to accept it led the Franco-Moroccan, Franco-Tunisian, and Franco-Guinean accords rapidly to disaster. More influential than the political contexts, which, here and there, were not likely to facilitate relations between France and her successive partners, was the triumph of the monetarist thesis at the conclusion of the agreements on the evolution of relations with the latter. An iron-collar monetary zone is, by definition, an improper framework for a mechanism of co-operation. Perfectly conceivable in a dependent community where relationship of power and economic satellitism persist, it is unacceptable in a Community founded on the principle of mutual development, on a real solidarity that refuses to subordinate some—even the weakest—to interests of the others. By rejecting this prospect, the franc zone was doomed to the deplorable splits that have developed, and the Franco-Malian experiment would enjoy no happier fate if it tried to ignore this lesson of recent history. In the contractual Community, since the france zone is basically one of growth and development, Mali has—to compensate for the limitations on sovereignty imposed by membership in the same zone of solidarity—a certain number of facilities necessary to its progress. It enjoys, by agreement, a real control over the central organisms of the zone, which can no longer unilaterally impose serious decisions or confront the other partners with a *fait accompli* in monetary matters.

In this connection, we may refer to Chapter IV of the agreement on the co-ordination of monetary policies, especially Article 25, which stipulates: "Any modification of the parity between the currency used in Mali and the French franc will be effected only after agreement between the two parties." And, furthermore, "The government of the French Republic will consult the government of the Mali Federation prior to any eventual negotiations of relations between the franc and foreign currencies and will negotiate with it measures to safeguard the legitimate interests of the Mali Federation." If the Federation agrees to utilize the French Institute of Issue, it is assured of an effective voice by participating in the naming of agency directors, and by exercising a right to check on the administration of the bank through the intermediary of the Monetary Commission, whose members it designates. In fact, Mali assumes direction of the credit policy, of the control of foreign exchange, and of capital movements —important advantages that other independent states have been able to obtain only after violent ruptures. The Malian Credit Council orients Mali's credit policy, formulates recommendations, makes decisions, informs the government by communications from the Central Bank concerning the evolution of bank deposits, banking applications, rediscount operations, banking risks in various kinds of activities, and foreign transfers (Article 28). It can, independently of its prescribed functions, exercise within the territory of the Federation the prerogatives assigned to it by the higher Credit Council. If it wishes, the government of the Federation will be represented not only on the Monetary Commission of the franc zone, but on the other common organisms, such as the Committee on Foreign Investments, the Committee on Economic and Financial Affairs, the Commission on Trade Agreements, and "all multilateral bodies dealing with economic and financial matters" (Article 34). Article 24 specifies that both parties reserve the right, at any moment, to terminate the established monetary regime "if this regime should seem to either party contrary to the defense of its legitimate interests." And, in this case in order to avoid brutal, unilateral decisions caused by temperamental outbursts that have no place in economic relations, it provides a review procedure with a cooling-off period for the study of the reform and its method of application.

To affirm the solidarity of the zone, it is not enough to co-ordinate the currencies; one must also co-ordinate the foreign-trade and finance policies. The provisions in Chapter III anticipate this. To remain faithful to its unifying mission, Mali felt obliged to recall once again, in its agreements with France, its attachment to the Customs Union of the West African States. In fact, Mali is convinced that there can be no economic and industrial development if an anachronistic, shortsighted protectionism erects customs barriers between the West African countries, whose interest is to establish a common market as soon as possible. In its relations with the French Republic, there will be a preferential regime and an acceptance of consultative procedures on import plans and international agreements with other countries. Foreign-exchange regulations of the franc zone will apply throughout the Federation, but Mali will exercise control delegated by the central monetary authorities to the federal authorities, who will name directors of the various offices. For its transactions outside of the franc zone, Mali has available a dollar account, accounts in other currencies, and credits in the amount of cash receipts and cash gifts and loans that it may obtain from international organizations or from foreign countries. It may receive a supplementary allocation of rights to draw on the currency reserves of the zone, calculated globally for each category of currency, with due regard for the needs of the totality of members of the zone and for the development plan of each territory.

In addition, the agreements wisely create a Franco-Malian Commission—with equal representation from each country—to guarantee a permanent liaison. The Commission is empowered to deal with all problems concerning Franco-Malian co-operation: to co-ordinate, on the one hand, trade and financial policies and, on the other, currency policies. Thus the Commission decides, by joint action, the exceptions to the preferential regime that Mali's developmental needs may require. It arbitrates in cases of disagreement between the director and technical adviser of the Exchange Office; it determines which operations, and in what amounts, should be charged to the supplementary drawing rights. Questions of currency reform and interpretation of the agreements are referred to the Commission. Finally, without going into detail, the agreement poses the principle of French assistance to Mali. Article 10 of Chapter II states: "Aid from the French Republic to the Mali Federation will consist primarily in the preparation of analyses, the furnishing of equipment, the sending of experts and technicians, the granting of financial assistance." Article 11 refers the methods and amounts to agreements to be negotiated subsequently.

On this point we should express ourselves clearly. Mali, which accepts the monetary policy previously discussed, professes the same policy with respect to foreign aid. This must cease being a kind of charity offered to ease the conscience of the wealthy, or a gift intended to ensure influence, political or economic—in other words, a new instrument of enslavement. On the contrary, it must be one of the factors to stimulate mutual development without ulterior motive, without reservation, without miscalculation, and without haggling. If it is really to be a means of effective development, assistance can no longer be granted according to the old routine of the dominant economy—the old-style technical assistance, drop by drop, to operations arbitrarily chosen from a list drawn up without previous planning. Assistance must be global, to allow not the execution of isolated projects singled out by the donor according to the imperatives of his own policy, but rather to help realize a dynamic plan prepared in view of a development that transcends personalities and regimes. For the same reasons, the global-aid formula must apply not only in our relations with France, but also with countries of the East or West, which, as is well known, wish to develop a strategy of domination by means of economic and financial aid. We shall have an opportunity to return to this point later.

Considering at the moment the question of eventual assistance from France, we must warn that though the conception and form of this aid are determined by developmental needs, a certain number of obligations are no less incumbent on the beneficiary: that of accepting frank and honest consultation to permit the harmonization of policies; that of respecting engagements freely contracted without any spirit of trickery; that of referring to bilateral negotiation the procedure for utilizing credits. It is important to make certain that these credits will not be diverted from their stated purpose, which is exclusively to finance the development plan. It will be necessary to admit, in the interest of the beneficiary and to give the donor legitimate guarantees, the possibility of blocking credits to prevent large, unproductive expenditures or the use of these resources to balance the budget. Such practices must be considered completely immoral in so far as international solidarity is concerned.

This summary analysis of the economic and financial agreements will inspire some to speak of excessive generosity and others to talk of compromises, even of compromise with imperialism. It is a fact that no solution can reconcile extremes. Middle roads are by definition those followed by men of the center and not of the extremes. By adopting the solution of co-operation in mutual development, we are sure, in Mali, that we have chosen for our people—and for the African peoples who will not be insensitive to our example—the best road, because it leads to a dual integration of the economy, first on the continental scale, and then on the world scale.

Mali and the Dual Integration

As a regional link, Mali's vocation is in fact to permit this dual integration and, first, to realize a continental economy. To remain faithful to this vocation, Mali has not seen fit—for purely national satisfactions—to break the economic and financial ties that link it to West African states. This, as we have already said, is one of the reasons for its decision to remain in the franc zone—a renovated franc zone. This is one of the reasons for refusing to mint our own money and to have our own central bank. This is one of the reasons for accepting a minimum number of common institutions, to assure the co-ordination of economic, financial, and foreign-trade policies. This is one of the reasons for attaching importance to the consolidation of the customs union and to the sacrifices that Mali is willing to make for it. Mali knows that its mission will not be fulfilled on the day when it will have built on its national territory a strong, progressive economy—even a wholly socialized economy according to a process of harmonious development—if it is surrounded by fragile economies with archaic structures, subject to the domination of foreign economies, capitalist or socialist. It recognizes the inadequacy of such a result, which would have no other advantage than to create a fringe of prosperity in an economic and social area where poverty and inhumanity are the fundamental characteristics. Mali aspires, on the contrary, to spread its development process throughout the continent, scorning artificial borders and the formalistic procedures of elemental nationalisms.

Animated by the growing developmental poles of the sister economy, Mali's economy will itself become the pole of all African economy, placing at the service of the latter its developmental dynamics, its traffic network, its trade, and its resources. Instead of setting itself up in competition, it will insist primarily on the complementary nature of African economies, on the necessity for co-operation and the duty of African nations to achieve equilibrium within the continent. This is why one of its principal aims will be the co-ordination of the various national plans and the acceptance by all African states of a master development plan, somewhat similar to the Colombo Plan. Such a project requires the pooling of the principal energy and mineral resources, a continent-wide industrialization. It also requires the denationalization of poles of development, which will be placed at the disposal of the ensemble. In concrete terms, this means that North African industrial complexes, the complex of Konkouré,[4] and the future propulsive units in Mali, Mauritania, and elsewhere will cease being factors of national development and become

[4] The Konkouré Dam in Guinea.—Tr.

125

factors of economic integration. This also means that the oil and phosphates of Mali, the oil and manganese of Gabon, the phosphates of Benin, will be exploited according to a definite plan taking into account the needs of the entire continent.

The utilization of an African Colombo Plan also implies the obligation upon foreign investors to pool the necessary capital, to co-ordinate technical assistance and methods of prospecting—in brief, to replace competition with an indispensable collaboration of the great powers. It is a multi-national aid that will foster harmonious development of African economy, in a climate of co-operation instead of struggle, to conquer new markets and new economic areas. One of Mali's basic objectives will be to favor, by all possible means, an African common market. First, a common market for agricultural output, which alone will enable us to face foreign markets that are organizing or already organized; to foster a policy of stabilization that largely conditions the development of African agriculture and the living standard of its workers. Does one need to insist on the potential in a common organization of African producers of peanuts, coffee, cacao, bananas, and different kinds of wood? The products of extractive industry will also be able to foster the organization of a common market that will assure its re-valorization by persuading producers of raw materials to present themselves—no longer separately, but as a united front—before foreign capitalism.

In all probability, for a long time to come it will be desirable and even necessary to appeal to private groups to organize African markets of mining products. But we deem it no less indispensable, in order that the idea may not be diverted from its true aim and serve to assure capitalists of monopolies —and this must be seriously stressed—to be careful to entrust the states themselves with the initiative for forming firms to exploit the pooled resources. These firms will thus become state companies in which private capital participates—multi national, even supranational companies. This makes even more apparent the need not only to co-ordinate fiscal and customs policies, but to create a general investment code to serve as the common charter of the various national codes. The creation of a market for African products will surely contribute more effectively to Africa's economic independence than nebulous theories and anticolonialist resolutions. True enough, to attain these different objectives it will not suffice to adopt a violently anti-imperialist attitude, or to gargle slogans that inflame the masses. It will not suffice to proclaim a verbal attachment to African unity and independence. It will require less eloquence, less destructive genius, and more concrete, positive facts. The facts will drive the phrase-mongers into a corner and exact from them a little more collective discipline, a few more collective sacrifices. It is on this condition that African independence will stop being a myth and become a de-mystified reality. In short, if co-operation is indispensable between the industrial and technical world powers in their assistance to African countries, a fortiori it must be the rule for the latter in their efforts to develop African economy as a vast ensemble. Economic co-operation, as well as technical and scientific co-operation, will make scientific and technical research an inter-African affair. Cultural co-operation will make great African universities—French or English-speaking—centers of cultural exchange, focal points for encounters between inter-African national elites.

127

In our opinion, it is by friendly, fraternal co-operation—on all levels—and not by solutions that are violent in deed or word that the inevitable integrations of African nations will be progressively realized, without injury for some, without pretentiousness for others; without enslavement for some, and without greed for power on the part of others.

As a pilot region, Mali holds her economy open to the world. It is ready for the dialogue with the nations of East and West, provided they do not ask it to give up its friends, to break its engagements as a member of a solidarity zone. Moreover, this would be a poor approach to the problem; a healthy comprehension of the evolution of relations between nations must carry with it a new perspective, no longer that of dialectical opposition, but of complementarities, of concentric solidarities. Viewed in this light, the East-West duality becomes complementary, within a zone of solidarity enlarged to worldwide dimensions. What was once irreconcilable opposition becomes a possibility of conciliation—better still, a *raison d'être* for an enriching coexistence and a factor of mutual development.

A relay station on the road toward world economy, Mali's economy opens first on Europe: first—why conceal it?—on the Six of the European Common Market. Historically, its first contacts have been with Europe; with Europe it has developed exchanges—good or bad, to its detriment or not. From Europe has come, until now, the most important financial and technical assistance. In Europe are implanted the axes of trade that Mali plans to use for its development, and the focal points of culture to which it has appealed in the past. Willingly or unwillingly, it is the European cultural, economic, and technical presence that is felt almost everywhere in Mali, if not

128

everywhere in Africa. This influence cannot be rejected a priori. But neither can it be adopted as it is, because of prior historical events. This history carries with it certain responsibilities, all of which do not reflect favorably on it. New grounds will be needed to justify our confidence, the shaken confidence of the Africans. Europe also needs to be reconverted, to stop being imperialistic, to cease to be the heroine of mercantile capitalism and to transform herself into the heroine of co-operation between economies that complement each other and are not subordinate one to the other. Europe must stop considering the African market as an outlet and the African continent as an appendage. She must understand once and for all that no project of a dominant capitalism, however well camouflaged, can permanently seduce the African countries.

Learning from past failures, Europe—and in this case, the Six of the European Common Market—must offer Mali a contract in the same spirit and on the same model as that negotiated wtih the former Metropole, for technical, economic, and financial co-operation. This would imply, on the part of the European associates, a more definite unity of economic policies respecting the *Tiers-Monde,* especially the African countries in the same zone of solidarity. It would imply a clearer doctrine concerning foreign aid and, in general, less equivocal attitudes. It will especially be necessary for Europe to favor transformations that the present evolution of Eurafrican relations requires. The enlargement of the co-operative zone to Europe supposes that Europe agrees to reorganize along the same lines, in the direction of mutual development, and in pursuit of the same aims, particularly toward becoming a regional link on the road to a world

129

economy. The authorities of the European Common Market, and especially those in Brussels, must answer these questions clearly to allow the beginning of a dialogue that deserves to be engaged.

To become an effective partner in the context of the new co-operation, Europe must make an effort to be true to herself, to be truly Europe; to build a continental economy, itself a zonal link; to become no longer a Europe of coalitions, a Europe divided into blocs, reduced to satellite rank and seeking compensation in imperialisms as illusory as they are camouflaged. In other words, an old land of liberty, civilization, and refined culture, Europe—which, despite our difficulties with her, still has a place in our affections—will have to free herself of her restraints and proceed with her revolution. A united Europe, "sans rivages,"[5] can—within the perspective of a world economy—contract a valid alliance with an Africa united "sans rivages," according to an elementary homothetic law. A Europe organized not on the basis of co-existence between capitalism and socialism, but on that of renovated socialism transcending the established orthodoxies, can hold a dialogue usefully with an Africa freed and organized along the same lines. In a word, the new orientation of Africa calls for a total reconversion of Europe. Professor Maurice Byé reaches a similar conclusion:

By creating their industry and agriculture, and allying their industry to their agriculture, underdeveloped countries will necessarily be organized economies. Could these organized economies flourish in a world entirely disorganized—in a

[5] *Europe sans rivages* is the title of a work by Professor Perroux, who suggests "Europe Unbounded by the Seas" as a suitable English translation.—Tr.

130

world that is merely the setting for free trade and for the creation of incentive by a pure and perfect market? Organized economies can flourish only in an organized world.

The consequences seem to me important and serious. The immersion of underdeveloped countries—which will necessarily be countries that plan their development and especially their agricultural development, a fact that almost no one disputes—the immersion of underdeveloped countries in a purely cosmopolitan, liberal, free-trade economic ensemble makes it impossible for them to attain their objectives. How can one expect to guarantee the development of agriculture if prices fluctuate excessively; if the markets are too uncertain; if industrial complementarities are subjected to the whim of world competition? The two things are incompatible. Unless we are careful, we may be heading from a universe divided by meridians, by what was called a shortage of dollars—distinguishing the Western from the Eastern hemisphere—toward a world divided by parallels. Then the underdeveloped countries—which are principally tropical economies, taking shelter in their quotas, in their controlled trade, in their barriers, making their plans for isolation— would attempt to cure their ills in a closed system. No doubt they would find support in other closed economies of Eastern Europe, planned economies like their own. In any event, the world would be divided between North and South.[6]

It is precisely a question of helping to reweld the blocs, of reconciling the opposing camps, of doing everything possible to avoid the irreparable—that is, "the rupture of the world between North and South." Mali's economy can contribute to this on condition that it does not have to act alone, on condition that it is the point of departure for a vast co-operative movement, drawing in its train the emergent African econ-

[6] Lecture on "Agriculture and Development," in *Chambres d'Agriculture* (March 15, 1960), p. 9.

omies—not because this is Mali's will, but because it is in the best interest of the African peoples, and because this is the mission that they must share with all nations of good will that accept the dialogue to resolve their common difficulties. Needless to say, these prospects are not immediate realities, otherwise they would cease to be prospects. What we are trying to show, in this age of speed where events surprise even the quickest minds, is the necessity for all, especially for Western Europe—always our partner—to understand that the time has come to make a change. And we Africans must realize that it would be criminal to miss Africa's hour because of sordid rivalries. Concretely, it is necessary for Western Europe, where nations and fatherlands are threatened by monopolistic capitalism—in the sense that François Perroux understands it—to proceed to a review of relations between economic and financial powers, to institute effective controls over the great firms and financial groups that depend on an outmoded liberalism to perpetuate their hegemony. It is a question of reforming the structure of world trade to enable countries of retarded growth to increase their exports, and of rearranging the regime of overpricing to assure mutual advantages in international trade. For the young African states, particularly for Mali, it is a question of resolutely taking the road to a "relay economy" that cannot be a liberal, but a socialist, transnationalist economy, accepting neither the war of the blocs nor the parceling of nations.

TOWARD A COMMUNITY OF
UNITED NATIONS

WHETHER THE DISGUISED IMPERIALISMS approve or not, the age of resignation has ended for the peoples and nations of the *Tiers-Monde*. They are no longer willing for others to think and decide for them. From now on they intend to think for themselves and make their own decisions. They are determined to take their own initiative in every field. Neither ideologies of power nor ideologies of submissiveness, proposed by illustrious apostles, can overcome their resolve. Even if gigantic forces should be mobilized to mutilate populations and plunge nations and homelands into mourning, no material force can destroy what is today the ideal of those nations and fatherlands. One may appeal to the moderating virtues of the great religions—to Christian brotherhood or to Moslem obedience. But it would be impossible to stifle the resentment of the hungry masses of the *Tiers-Monde*, Christian or Moslem, or to prevent the explosion of their anger in a world where the most modern societies, the most advanced technically, are also the most barbaric, the most inhuman.

But to be creative, the twentieth-century revolution must be something other than a revolt against hunger or a proletarian riot. It must be more than a class revolution on the scale of nations and of continents; it must be a world revolution,

133

affecting the totality of nations and continents. Naturally, neither the classical Marxist formulas, nor even less the models of the capitalist system, permit such a prospect, which requires a complete break with the distorted analyses to which the leading orthodoxies have accustomed us. In this phase of historical change, it is necessary to renovate everything: prospects, concepts, and methods of attacking problems, including the dialectical method, which must undergo a healthy readaptation. The revolution in question is, above all else, an intellectual revolution, challenging the ideological system and the results it has produced. Technological successes registered here and there are unfortunately too technical and, in any case, too limited for one to judge their effectiveness as instruments of universal progress. Perhaps it would be better to have, I shall not say less intelligence, but certainly less technological success and more human progress.

This may be the moment to remind Intelligence of the respect that she owes man, if she wishes to survive her present glory. This is also the moment to remind the great modern civilizations that their permanence, or simply their continuance, does not depend on their brilliance, but rather on their human content, on their capacity for human progress. "Civilizations," notes Gabriel Ardant, "have always perished because of their narrowness—physical or intellectual; in other words, from their failure to include the more numerous masses of men, with whom they have been unable to share their progress."[1] Failing to understand this, despite the glory that they have known, mercantile civilizations, from the Roman Empire to Carthage, have crumbled one by one. Modern civilizations will not experience a better fate, notwithstanding

[1] *Op. cit.*, Introduction.

technical advancement and extraordinary scientific contributions, if they remain narrowly limited physically and intellectually. But why prophesy, since they already show so many signs of decline, precisely because they lack the necessary breadth of vision and do not provide themselves with a framework of world-wide dimensions?

It is symptomatic that our era, which is that of guided missiles, is also the era of the greatest crisis the world has known; and the most technically advanced nations are far from secure. Science will really become a boon to all mankind only when it stops being an instrument enabling some to dominate others. Technical development will really become a crucial factor for progress only when it is within the reach of every nation, large or small, rich or poor. In short, the fundamental law of the new world is essentially co-operative. The civilization to be born will only know durable progress through scientific co-operation that will ban monopolies of national states and restore science to its universal status; and through technical co-operation that will place the most modern techniques of development at the disposal of the most backward countries by utilizing appropriate formulas of assistance. Without this co-operation between the nations of all continents, of all ages, of all ideological formations, making inventions and discoveries the property of all humanity and not exclusively that of particular nations, the progress of science and technology will only be able to hasten world disintegration by increasing the disparities and disequilibriums.

There is no reason to be pessimistic if one is determined to play the game, to use the advantages at one's disposal, to build on the ruins of the dying mercantile civilization a new one, more human, better balanced. Furthermore, it is essential that rivalry in a tormented, torn universe give way to co-operation; not verbal co-operation interested only in propaganda, but effective, sincere co-operation that—eliminating the causes of conflicts and armed disputes—would convince everyone of the uselessness of expenditures on armament, which divert so many resources from tasks of collective creation. From this will to collaborate must emerge a unanimous agreement to co-operate, especially in the peaceful use of the new nuclear science, which, under these conditions, remains the great hope of our century, the one tool powerful enough to solve the problems of our time. Thus it will be less a question of discrediting science and technology than of requiring the powers that wish to monopolize scientific and technological progress to submit to the law of solidarity. This law expropriates from individual nations for the profit of the Community of Nations.

The Community of Nations is, in short, the ultimate stage of the evolution now appearing faintly here and there in the form of communities restricted by affinities. This is the final phase toward which the building of the new civilization should lead. In various places, dialogues are fashioning this new civilization, the vocation of which is to be "a civilization of solidarity." We shall stress forcefully the fact—without indulging in demagoguery—that the nations of the *Tiers-Monde*, especially the emergent African nations, are required, as much as the old nations, to obey this fundamental law of our age, at the risk of having only a very brief history.

Epilogue

THE FEDERATION OF MALI
TESTED BY THE FACTS

If there is an especially risky undertaking today, it is surely that of writing. Our world is moving so swiftly that what seemed perfectly true three months ago is now completely false; and the constructions that are apparently the most logical, the most durable, crumble like castles of cards. We were hoping to present Mali as an example of inter-African solidarity, a living testimonial to international co-operation. Since the rupture of the Federation on the night of August 19–20, 1960, we have been compelled to renounce this ambition. Nevertheless, we have been unwilling to suppress or even to alter the references to Mali in this volume. At least this will be a testimonial to our good faith, even if it reveals the extent of our credulity. We take consolation in being able, thanks to the chronology of events, to offer our readers a critique of the model of solidarity that we were proposing to the world. Our fundamental option can only be strengthened thereby.

CRITIQUE OF THE MALI-MODEL ZONE OF SOLIDARITY

The issue here is not the theory of solidarity nor the need for African unity. Nor is the policy of large groupings contradicted by the events. At most, one can claim that the rupture of Mali refutes our theories on the formation of the African nation and our theses on the process of setting up large economic complexes. It clearly indicates the failure of the ways and means that we preferred, as well as the schemata of historical evolution that we favored. Theoretically, a federation presupposes the existence of two or more states, with distinct personalities. In fact, by reinforcing the central power, the federation tends to stifle the personality of the states that compose it. Not unreasonably, numerous specialists in international law have shown what is artificial and theoretical in the commonly accepted distinction between a classic federation and a unitary state. In this connection, two typical examples come to mind: the Soviet Union and the United Arab Republic.

In Mali we hoped to avoid the disadvantages inherent in federal structures by imagining an original legal structure, halfway between a federation and a confederation. Perhaps we built an attractive thesis and elaborated a satisfactory model for a creation in abstract law. But we did not produce a creation in real law. Stronger than constitutional provisions, more imperative than legal nuances, the facts forced evolution to follow its usual curve. It is useless to erect guardrails to prevent trespassing; it is pointless to multiply warnings and lectures to preserve the internal sovereignty of states and maintain a necessary equilibrium between the powers involved. By the very nature of things, the centralizing tendency, gaining strength as the institutions are set up, will triumph over constitutional rules and the partners' repeated avowals to respect the affiliated entities. As is always the case in like circumstances, the central power, concentrated in the hands of one of the partners, soon becomes a terrible instrument of

138

domination, weighing heavily on the territory of the state where it is located—in this instance, on the territory of Senegal. The theoretically bipartite character of the Mali government could not check this evolution, which was in the logic of history.

Inasmuch as the thesis of the installation of a chief executive distinct from the prime minister prevailed against the thesis of a concentration of powers, we could hope that the danger of absorption of one state by the other—of Senegal by the Sudan—was finally eliminated, because of the apparatus of the federal state. This underestimated the strength of the centralizing tendency, the greed for power that secretly gnaws at many African leaders, even when they call themselves democrats. The designation of the president of the republic could not fail to arouse a violent manifestation of this desire for political conquest, which was barely concealed from the outset. Once the thesis of concentration of powers was eliminated and a regime of arbitration instituted, the only way to be master of this arbitration, to bend it toward a policy of domination rather than co-operation, was to seize the supreme office or else to install a personality on whom one could count in advance. Though nothing could excuse the disloyalty of brothers pledged to co-operate in a spirit of brotherhood for the success of an admittedly difficult common undertaking, it must be conceded that the Senegalese situation could mislead foreign observers insufficiently informed about the complexity of Senegalese realities and unfamiliar with local psychology. Judging by appearances, the supporters of the thesis of absorption thought all the conditions favored their offensive. Ensuing events were to prove their calculations false.

On the Senegalese side, the leaders who were the principal

theoreticians of African unification and who, on various occasions, had sacrificed their local political organization and personal position to this idea, bear undeniable responsibilities, though they acted in good faith. Their error—our error—has been that in our fight against Balkanization, we failed to consider the precolonial fact that is territorialism. Our mistake has been our failure to pay sufficient attention in our analyses to this phenomenon, a fruit of colonialism and sociopolitical fact that a theory of unity—no matter how praiseworthy or attractive—cannot abolish. We allowed ourselves to be lured by the mirage of the most intellectually satisfying construction. Taking our ideal for a reality, we thought we had only to condemn territorialism and its natural product, micronationalism, to overcome them and assure the success of our chimerical undertaking.

As a matter of fact, the Senegalese masses adopted the Mali mystique only because they were attached to their leaders. Their adherence to Mali was merely a new act of faith in their leaders. Senegalese territorialism was still alive, all the more so because the Sudanese presence in Dakar was too indiscreetly manifest to let the people forget it. This fact explains why, instead of arousing regrets, the rupture of the Federation was welcomed with relief by the masses, and no support to maintain the Federation was forthcoming anywhere. The Sudanese, very Malian in Dakar—or so they pretended—were no less territorialists. Though they talked Mali a lot, they thought Sudan and reacted above all as Sudanese. With a slant less Malian than Sudanese they studied problems that were properly Malian, especially problems related to defense, justice, education, and the Africanization of cadres. In such matters, the most Malian of the Sudanese supported the views of the Sudanese Union[1] much more than those of the Party of African Federation.[2] The latter, despite its other territorial sections, was reduced, because of Mali's bilateral structure, to narrow bipartitism, with all the difficulties of so limited a dialogue. The bipartite structure explains why the Party of African Federation, notwithstanding its affirmed vocation as a unifier, was unable to unify, reconcile, or arbitrate. Itself a hotbed of tensions and a fiction from birth, it could neither offer the slightest chance of mediation nor play a stabilizing role. From the structural point of view, it was too weak to serve as a political support. Definite proof of this was furnished by its ineffectiveness during the Mali crisis, which it was unable to survive. One can wonder what right the Sudanese had to decide its dissolution unilaterally. But it is difficult not to note that fact and not to list the particulars of its demise, however attached one might be to the idea of political regrouping.

In our opinion, it is in the maze of these various contradictions that one must seek the underlying causes of the breakup of the Federation. An emotional analysis would concern itself mainly with personalities, which, though not without significance, are nonetheless tangential and might make one overlook the essential phenomena. The temptation is strong—and naturally has not been resisted—to seek a scapegoat, to designate the traditional scapegoat: "colonial imperialism." This accusation, to which many so happily resort, must be vigorously denounced, for it is merely an attempt to mystify world opinion and is totally devoid of intellectual honesty. In

[1] The *Union Soudanaise* was the Sudanese political party headed by Modibo Keïta, who served as prime minister of the Mali Federation.—Tr.
[2] The *Parti de la Fédération Africaine*, of which Léopold Sédar Senghor was president, had sections in Senegal, Sudan, Dahomey, etc.—Tr.

the case of Mali, we must contend that the charge is reactionary and retrograde, inasmuch as we feel that it represents a refusal to criticize oneself and a deliberate determination to be right in spite of the facts. It is too easy to excuse the errors and mistakes, the failure of a policy for which one is entirely responsible, by imputing these to so-called colonialist maneuvers that in one's conscience one knows to be purely imaginary, but which always impress anticolonialist circles. Our indignation is all the greater because those very persons who called in vain for the intervention of French troops against a Senegalese government defending Senegalese independence have set themselves up as accusers and as victims after the failure of their attempt. We are distressed to observe that in anticolonialist circles, pigheadedness has been able to kill the critical spirit to such an extent that all analyses of African problems are basically falsified by stands taken a priori, which have no connection with anything progressive. These stands, on close examination, reflect a paternalism as intolerable as the paternalism that we denounce in the colonialists. This attitude disconcerts African progressives, who have long been cured of any complex and who refuse to take orders from any source other than what they believe to be in the interest of their country; and who do not make anticolonialism —or anti-France—a billboard advertisement.

A TIMELY REVISION

Instead of taking refuge in a romantic martyrdom, instead of proudly contradicting the facts, it seems to us more reasonable to revise our conceptions, to correct our methods, while remaining true to our aims. This is the least that can be expected of those who take pride in their Marxist training. As a matter of fact, Marx, who was scientific, readily yielded to the rigor of facts and did not hesitate, whenever it became necessary, to revise his position on a given political problem of his time. First an antifederalist—for reasons that half-baked Marxists today pick up and transpose *mutatis mutandis*—he quickly qualified his opinion and admitted the federal solution along with the right of self-determination. Why should others not be allowed, by the force of events, to change from an acceptance of federalism to the rejection of federalism, at least temporarily? Federation, like other forms of regrouping, is not an end in itself. It is a means, and like any other means, can prove itself only by its effectiveness. We should not worship it blindly, for this would make us deaf to the lessons of history; this would lead us to act against the basic interests of our people, of our countries.

We were defenders of federalism, but we need not be fanatics, since obviously its time has not yet come and since we are faced with micronationalisms that need to be tamed, micronations that will have to be organized. Thus it is necessary for us to start with these micronationalisms and micronations, which are the realities of this strange twentieth-century African universe. Then we can build modestly, gradually, the bases of a great African nationalism and the foundations of a great African nation. From now on, we shall be lucid enough to admit that if such be the final phase of a patient, historical development, we must anticipate the stages, prepare for the transitions, take into consideration sociologies that are different though apparently analogous, and neutralize the selfishness of the groups in power. Thus prepared, we shall then be able to shoulder our responsibilities with the certainty of reaching the final goal and of pursuing on realistic bases the task of regrouping.

The fulfillment of this task will be facilitated by this revision that places it beyond myths and finally within reach of the hands that fashion history. Instead of being compromised by the rupture of the Mali Federation, the task of regrouping faces new opportunities, immense prospects along the road to multinational co-operation on the basis of national independences. In so far as each takes care to respect the national policy of its neighbor—provided that policy conforms to the Charter of the United Nations; in so far as each forgoes increasing its influence to the detriment of others, or growing at the expense of the ensemble; in so far as the security of all is guaranteed by the absolute loyalty of the partners, co-operation will cease to be a wish and become common practice. To prepare for the future, it will be limited to a flexible co-ordination of national policies in areas already indicated: economic, social, cultural, and technical. This co-operation can henceforth be established without discrimination between East African and West African states, whatever the zone of linguistic influence and, above all, whatever the difference of ideological orientation.

It is on this condition that the African continent will change its vocation entirely and stop being—despite declarations of independence—an open arena for foreign competition and the Cold War. Only on this condition can Africa become a pilot continent, an example of a zone of continental solidarity. It is pertinent to add here that the application of this policy of co-operation on the continental scale presupposes complete decolonization—from the Mediterranean to the Cape of Good Hope, from the Indian Ocean to the Atlantic—and therefore the acceleration of the movements to liberate peoples still dominated: those of Algeria, Angola, Mozambique, Kenya, and South Africa. The total elimination of colonialism can only make co-operation more fruitful, by focusing on concrete problems of development, that is, on building a continental civilization.

In this connection, the demise of the Mali Federation must not be mourned with funereal tom-toms, but deserves to be heralded as a great day dawning on a continent quivering with hope.